Ad Illustrator

Art of Graphic Creation Art Working and Illustration

(The Complete Beginners Manual With Latest Tips & Tricks to Master)

Herbert Oliver

Published By **Bengion Cosalas**

Herbert Oliver

All Rights Reserved

Adobe Illustrator: Art of Graphic Creation Art Working and Illustration (The Complete Beginners Manual With Latest Tips & Tricks to Master)

ISBN 978-1-7775976-7-2

Legal & Disclaimer

The information contained in this book is not designed to replace or take the place of any form of medicine or professional medical advice. The information in this book has been provided for educational & entertainment purposes only.

The information contained in this book has been compiled from sources deemed reliable, and it is accurate to the best of the Author's knowledge; however, the Author cannot guarantee its accuracy and validity and cannot be held liable for any errors or omissions. Changes are periodically made to this book. You must consult your doctor or get professional medical advice before using any of the suggested remedies, techniques, or information in this book.

Table Of Contents

Chapter 1: Adobe Illustrator Cc

Adobe Illustrator CC is the Premier Vector drawing application create shapes Composed of Points, lines and Curves that are stored as mathematical instruction as opposed to a bitmap application, which creates shapes composed of pixel dots. A wide array of print and screen designers use to illustrator to create design and Artwork.

Application Frame

The entire Illustrator interface is housed within the Application frame.

Mac OS: The Application frame is displayed by default.

To show the Application frame,

choose Window > Application Frame.

A check mark will appear next to the command and the frame will appear onscreen. To minimize the frame in Mac OS, click the yellow Minimize button.

Windows:In Windows, the Application frame is always visible. To minimize the Application frame in Windows, click the Minimize button.

The Main interface elements in illustrator CC are as Follow

•The Control Panel

•The Application Bar

•The Tools panel

•Works Spaces

•Panels

•The Control Panel

The Panel Option Change Depending on the tool or type of Object. you can use this Panel to Apply fill and Stroke Colors; change an object Variable width profile, Brush Stroke definition, or opacity Apply basic Types Attributes; Align and distribute multiple object.

•Application Bar

Click the buttons on the Application bar. Choose options from the Arrange Documents menu to arrange multiple Document windows within the Application frame.

•The Tools panel

The Tools panel, also called the toolbar, contains tools used for selecting, drawing, and editing objects It also includes controls for choosing color, a menu for choosingone of three drawing modes, and a menu for choosing one of three screen modes.

Related tools are grouped together on the panel.Click a visible tool icon to select it. Hold down the mouse buttonon a tool that displays a tiny arrow to choose from hiddentools.Option-click (Mac OS) or Alt-click (Windows) a tool icon to cycle throughall the tools within its related group.

To quickly choose a tool, press the letter shortcut that is assigned to it.Keyboard shortcuts are listed in the tool tips that display when you place the pointer over a tool icon and in tool menus.

•Create Custom Tools Panels

For a more efficient drawing and editing workflow, you can create custom tools panels that contain only tools you use for specific tasks.

To create a free-floating custom tools panel:

1 Choose Window> Tools> New Tools Panel.

2 In the New Tools panel dialog box, enter a name for the new tools panel.

3 Click OK. t\ new, blank panel displays in the Applicationframe, containing Fill and Stroke buttons.

4Drag a tool from the default Tools panel into theupper area of the custom panel. When the pointer becomesan arrow head with a plus (+) symbol, release the mouse button. The tool icon will appear on the custom panel

5 Repeat this method to add additional tools to the custom panel.

6 To remove a tool from the custom panel, drag it out of the panel.

•Work spaces

Workspaces are customarrangements of thepanelsandpanelgroupsin the dock, alongwith any user-createdtools panels, floatingtear offtoolbars,andcustom tools panels.

On the Controlpanel,use theworkspace switchermenuto switchbetweenthese eightpredefined workspaces,As you displayeachworkspace,take noteof which panelsAdobe selected to support a specific designworkflow.

Create a Custom Work spaces

the panels at the beginning of each work session, you can create and save user-defined workspaces to various projects' design needs and your work style.

Forsome panels (suchas Color,Stroke, andCharacter)youcan display some or all option areasby clicking theverticalarrowtwoor threetimeson thepaneltab.

Rearrange panel & Dock

•To widen an expanded panel or dock, drag its side or bottom edge.

•To move a panel within its group, drag its tab left or right.

•To move a panel out of Its group in the dock, drag its tab Into a new group or between panel groups, and release the mouse button when the blue drop zone border or line appears.

To create a new vertical dock for panels, drag a panel tab or Icon over the vertical left edge or the dock and release the mouse button when the blue vertical drop zone bar appears. Drag other panel tabs or Icons into the new vertical dock, as desired.

Chapter 2: Working With Documents

Create a New Document

To get started on creating artwork in Illustrator, you'll first create a new document.

1 Choose File> New. The New Document dialog box opens

2 Enter a name for the new document in the Name field.

3 From the Profile menu, choose a profile that matches the output medium for which you are designing.For this exercise, choose Print.

6. Click the First Orientation button to specify that the art board is in Portrait orientations.

7. Expand the Advanced setting area, if necessary, and view the default settings for the Print profile you selected.

8. Click ok. A new document window opens

9. To place an object on your new document, display the Symbol panel, and drag any symbol onto the art board

Art boards

Every Illusuator document contains at least. one art boardor the dimensions special field In the New Document dialog box. The art board Is called the "live" area because any objects placed on that art board will output to your chosen output device or be exported with your final file.

A document can have multiple art boards or a uniform size or or different sizes. For example, you could create a document with customized Art board that each contain a businesscard, stationery, or a brochure for a client Identitypackage, A document with separately sized web graphics for a website project.

Using the illustrator Art board toolyou can edit your Art board at any time.

Add Artboards

You can add additional art boards to a document at any time.

1Select the Art board tool Icon or press Shlft+O.

2On the View menu, select SmartGuidesto show onscreen alignmentguides.

3 Hold the Command key (Mac OS) or Ctrl key (Windows) and press - (hyphen) to zoom out and view more of the canvas area In your document.

4Usingthe Artboard tool,drag Inthe canvas to create a new artboardUse the smart guides to help alignthe new artboard withan existing one.

Resize Artboards

•Click an art board to select it.

•Select a screen or paper size form the Paper menu

•Enter values in the W and H Fields

•Select a new orientation Button

Duplicate Artboards

•DUPLICATE WITHOUT THECONTENTS

•To   duplicatea   selectedanboardwithoutIts contents:

Using the Artboard panel: On the Artboards panel, clicka New Artboard Button to select the artboard you want to duplicate. Click the New Artboard button. The blank,duplicateArtboard Is added to the right. or theexiting Artboard.

DUPLICATE WITH THE CONTENTS

Using the Artboards panel:On the Artboards panel, clicka listingto select theariboardyou want. 10 duplicate. Dragthe selectedto theNew Artboard button. The duplicate artboard with contentsIs added to the right of theexciting artboards.

Delete an Artboard

Using the Artboards panel : on the Artboards panel, click the listing for the artboard you want to delete Artboard Button.

Save a Document

You can save an Illustrator file in six different formats

although we willfocus on the Adobe Illustrator(.ai)formatin thisexercise. Use the .al formatwhenyouplan to print thefiledirectly fromIllustrator or whenyouplanto importthefile into a program that can read the .al format,suchas AdobeIn Design.

1 To save a documentfor the firsttime,chooseFile> Save, or press Command+S (Mac OS) or Ctrl+S (Windows).

2 In the Save As (Mac OS) or File Name (Windows) field, enter a filename.

3 Navigate to the desired save folder.

4From the Format (Mac OS) OI' Save as Type (Windows)menu, choose the Adobe Illustrator(.ai) format. Click Save. The Illustrator Options dialog box opens.

5Click save

6Leave the Version menu set to Illustrator CC.

7 Verify that Create PDF Compatible Fileis selectedunder Options. Illustrarorsaves a PDF version(alongwiththe Illustrator data) that willallowapplications thatcan'tread Illustrator data to open anddisplaythe file.

8 Select Embed ICC Profiles to embed any color profile assigned to the file.

9 Select Use Compression to reduce the saved file's size.

10 Click OK The file is saved and will remain open in Illustrator, Keep your document open and proceed to the next task.

Ending a Work Session

To finish a work sessioninIllustrator:

1 Save and close each document that's open:

• To close each document, click the X on the documenttab nextto the file nameor press Command+W (Mac OS) or Ctrl+W(Windows).

• If the document contains unsaved changes, an alert displays. Click Save to preserve changes or Don'tSave to discard the latest changes.

2 When all the documents are closed, chooseIllustrator>Quit Illustrator (Mac OS) or File > Exit (Windows). You can also press Command+Q (Mac OS) or Ctrl+Q (Windows).

Chapter 3: Creating Basic Shapes

Basic Shapes

In Illustrator CC, you use the drawing tools on the Tools panel to create shapes.

A shape is a path that consists of straight and/or curved line segments connected by anchor points.The path on a shape can be open (as in a line or a spiral), or closed (as in a circle, which has no starting and ending point).Any created clement in an Illustrator document is also referred to as an object.

Create Shapes

First, let's create some basic shapes.

1 Create a new document by choosing File>New.

2 In the New Document dialog box, select Print from the Profile menu.

3 In the Number of Artboards field, type 3.

4 Select Letter from the Size menu. Specify any other desired settings, and click ok

5 Select the Rectangle tool (M)or the Ellipse tool

(L).

6 Drag diagonallyacross an artboard,and releasethe mouse button.

7 Draw several more rectangles and ellipses on the artboard. When you're finished, choose File> Save As to name and save your document. Leave it open.

Round Rectangle

Illustrator Provides a handy tool to

create a Rectangle with Round Corners.

1. Select the Round Rectangle Tool

Around Rectangle Shape Created.

Other Basic Shapes

Once you Create a shape, the Current fill and Stroke settings are applied and the shape remains selected for further modifications.

Polygon tool

1. Select the Polygon tool

2. Place the pointer where you want to locate the centre of the Shape and drag across an artboard. while dragging do the Following.

To Scale the polygon, drag away from or toward the center.

3. Release the Mouse button. the polygon shape is Selected.

To Create a Polygon by entering Values, click the polygon tool on an Art board. in the dialogue box that opens, enter Radius and slides value, and click ok.

Star tool

You can create a star by Dragging or clicking with the star tool.

You can Create a star by Dragging or clicking with the star tool.

1. Select the Star tool

2. Locate the pointer where you want to locate the center of the shape, and drag across an artboard.

3. Release the Mouse Button to create the star shape

The higher value create the outermost points. The greater the Difference between the two radios values ,the narrower the arms will be. Next, enter a points value to specify the number of points on the star and click ok.

Reshape Corner

The simplestway to reshapean object isto use theLiveShapes andLive Corners features to modifythecorners   of thepath.Thesetwofeaturesenableyouto   easily createdrounded   segments   on   oneorallof thecornerson a shape. Thefeatures are "live" becauseyoucanadjustor evenremovethecurvature of a corner pointat anytime.

CREATE A COPY USING THE SELECTION TOOL

To preserve your original geometric shape, you can create a copy of the object and reshape the copy.

1 Select the Selection tool.

2Option-drag (Mac OS) or Alt-drag (Windows) to copy an object and reposition the copy.

RESHAPE THE CORNERSOF A PATH USINGLIVE SHAPES

You can apply the Live Shapesfeatureto a rectangle or roundedrectanglewhen allthe pointson the object are selected.Live Shapes (and its widgets) will remain active for these types of objectseven if you scaleor rotatethe objects.

1Selectthe Selection tool.Do the following:

• Clickinside a rectangleor a roundedrectangle object that displaysa fill color.

2ChooseWindow>Transformto opentheTransform panel.

When a rectangle or rounded rectangle is selected, themiddle portion of the paneldisplays theRectangle(shape) Properties settings. These shape settings, along with the corner widgets, make up the Live Shapes feature.

3 Do any of thefollowing:

• Drag a corner widget inward to adjust the corner radius for all of the corners.(Remember, the entire object is selected.) To changethecorner style, Option-click(Mac OS) orAlt-click(Windows) anywidgetto cycle through thethreecornerstyles(round, inverted, or chamfer).

In the Transform Panel, in the Rectangle Properties area, click any arrow to adjust the corner radius. when the link corner radius value button is enable,all the corner are modified. you can click the link button to disable it,and adjust the corner radius value for a single corner.

Remove a Point

You can remove (delete) an anchorpointfrom the pathof any Illustratorobject.

In the following steps, you will create a triangle by simply removing a corner point from a rectangle.

1 Select a rectangle object.

2 Do the following:

• Select the Pen tool (P). Locate the pointer over a corner point on the rectangle, and click to removethe point.

Using either of these methods, the closed path will not be cut (meaning it will not become an open path).

You now have a three-corner object.

3Use the DirectSelection (A)toolto drag any of the segmentsor cornerpoints to reshapethe object.

You can also remove a point using the delete Anchor point tool. to select this tool. toHyphen (-) or click and hold the hiden tools and select it. Position the delete anchor Point tool over an Anchor point on a selected or unselected object, then click. the tool will not open a closed Path.

Chapter 4: Fill Stroke And Color

Working with fill and Stroke

You Can apply a variety of attributes to every object drawn in illustrator. The Two Most basic attributes are the fill color (inside color) and Stroke color (edge color) of the object's path. The stroke can have other settings to control its attributes such as the width and exact placement of the color on the path.

Change the Fill and Stroke Color

You can Modify the color of your newly created shapes at any time. You can use the Following methods to change the fill and strokes colors.

Apply Colors Via The Color Panel

1. using the Selection tool (V) Click an object in Your Document to Select it.

2. on the Color panel, select a color model From the Panel menu:

To define colors for Prints output,select Print CMYK. In this case,Your Illustrator document should have an output profile for Print.

To colors for video,web, or mobile device output,select RGB.

To specify a shade of gray, select grayscale.

3. Click the fill Square. Drag the color sliders to mix a color, or click the color spectrum bar.

4. click the stroke square and select a color using the color sliders or specturm bar.

Color Panel

Apply Stroke Attributes

You can only see the stroke (edge) of a path if it has a weight applied. The weight is expressed in points. Once you can see the stroke, you can change how it aligns with the path, select caps for its endpoints, and changethe cornerstyle.

APPLY A STROKEWEIGHT

You can modify a path'sstrokeweight(width) using the Stroke,Control, or Appear• ance panel. Modifyingthe stroke weighton one of these panelsupdatesthe setting on the othertwo panels automatically.

1Using the Selection tool ~ (V), click an objectto selectit.

2 Do either of the following:

• On the Control panel, enter a value in the Stroke Weightfield or clickthe up and down arrows to increaseor decreasethe currentstroke weight.

Applying a gradient or pattern to a selected object is a straightforward process. on the swatch panel, click to make the fill or stroke sqaure active, then click a gradient or pattern, click to apply it.

Recolor Art Work

The Recolor Artwork command displays a dialog box of option for changing the colors on multiple selected objects.This feature provides a powerful way to change colors Inan applied pattern, gradient, or solid color on selectedobjects.

1 Select. one or more objects. Their fill and stroke can contain patterns, gradients, or solid colors.

2 On the Control panel,click the Recolor ArtworkIcon Ii].

3 In the lower part of the Recolor Artwork dialog box, select Recolor Art. The following four sectionsexplain how to use the Recolor Artwork dialog box.

Save the Existing Artwork Colors

In the Recolor Artwork dialogue box, you can save the current colors applied to the objects

1 In the top part of the dialouge box, click the get colors from selected Art dropper and enter a descriptive name in the Name field.

2 click the new color Group icon. a color group is added to the color groups list.

Edit Colors using the Color wheel

You can modify colors with the color wheel in the Recolor Artworker dialouge box

1 click the Edit tab at left. colors from the selected artwork display as markers on a color wheel.

Chapter 5: Create Logo

Precise Alignment of objects

Illustrator provides nonprinting ruler guides and smart guides (both of which will not appear on paper or digital output) to help you position and aligned objects in your artwork.

A Primer on Guids

Ruler Guids

First, you will need to display rulers along the top and left sides of the document window. to do this, choose

View > Rulers > Show Rulers. Simply drag from either ruler into the document to place a ruler guide.

Guides are useful a aliment aids when positioning objects in your artwork. when the View > snap to point features is enabled, dragging any path edge, anchor point, or center point near a guide will cause that edge or point to snap to the guide.

Rular Guides remain visible onscreen until you opt to hide them. you can lock them, making them non selected and unable to be moved purposefully or accidently.

and you can unlock them, making them selectable and able to repositioned at any time.

To delete an unlocked guide, select it using a selection tool, then press Delete (Mac OS) or Backspace (Windows).

Smart Ruler

Smart Guids

Smartguidesproducenon printinglabelsandlines thattemporarilyappear onscreenwhen you drag to create,transform, or move an object.

You can use them to quickly align an object withnearbyedges,points, or centerpointsof other objects.Smartguides alsoappear when you create,resize,or repositionartboardsir Artboardmode.

Whenyou rollover a selectedor unselected object,smart guides will highlightits entirepathand display labels such as "path," "anchor," or "center"to designate wherethose elements are located.Measurement labelsalsoappearwhenyou roll over an anchorpointor draw an object.

You may choose View>Smart Guides, or press Command+U (Mac OS) or Ctrl+U (Windows) to turn thisfeature on and off.

Create a Basic Logo with Shape & Text.

01. Utilise the shape and Panel Tool

02. Duplicate elements and combine

To compare variants, duplicate a master copy to edit (hold Alt and drag). Create shapes to align objects and use Smart Guides (View>Smart Guides). Use the Pathfinder tool to combine shapes and create new ones. You can combine rectangles to make the 'H' element: select both elements and hit Merge.

03. Tweak the type

Alter the tracking and kerning of words to change the tone of a logo. Add character to the logotype by opening up the shapes into the native paths that make up the letters, altering the paths of each letter directly to make your type unique. To quickly convert the font to outlines (paths) hit Cmd/Ctrl+Shift O.

04. Time to add colour

In CS4 and higher, you can integrate Adobe's Kuler app into your workspace to view colour palettes. Go to Window > Extensions > Kuler. Try to avoid gradients in logos, but don't take that as an absolute rule. Hit Cmd/Ctrl+F9 to access the Gradient dialog. Try the logo on a variety of background colours and shapes.

05.Create a Delivery Templates

Go to File > Save As > Illustrator Template. Choose fonts that work well with the brand. Create style guides for designs: add CMYK colour breakdowns, Hex codes or Pantone codes, and font names – this is useful for designers and ensures brand consistency. Also give examples of the brand on various materials.

Apply Effect to an object

Youcan applyeffects,suchas DistortionandStlylastic changes,to anobject to produceresultsthatrange from subtle to pronounced. Effects are appliedusingthe Appearancepanelor the e.rrec1menu.

Effects change only the appearance of an object and notIts underlying path.You can edit or delete effects at any time without permanently altering the objectto which they are applied. You alsocan apply multiple effects to anobject and those effec1scan remain independentof each other.That is, a change10one effect willnot alter any othereffects.Betterstill, effects are live.Ifyoureshape the path of the underlying object, the effecaswill adjust accordingly.

1 Select an object, and do the following:

• From the Effect menu, select an Illustrator effect from the categories listedat the top.

Edit an Effect

You can editor remove effects at any time.

1 Select an objectthatcontainsan effect.

2 On the Appearance panel, click the underlinedeffect name.(If you nested the effect within the Stroke or Fill attribute, expandthatlisting to access the effect link.)

3In the dialog box thatopens,adjust any settingsor options, and click OK.

Save Effectsas Styles

On the Graphic Styles panel, you can save the currentsettings for an appliedeffect as a style for repeateduse.Effect settings saved as styles can be quickly appliedto otherobjects with one click.

1Selectan object that contains one or more effects.

2Choose Window>Graphic Styles to open the GraphicStyles panel. At the bottom of the panel, click the New Graphic Style icon. The current Stroke Fill, and effects settings of the selected object are saved as a style, and a new thumbnail appearson the GraphicStyles panelas the last thumbnail.

3Double-clickthe thumbnail,enter a namefor the style, and click OK to accept the new filename.

4To apply the saved style to anotherobject,select thatobject.On the Graphic Styles panel, click the graphicstyle's thumbnail.

Chapter 6: Live Paint

Live Paint a Feature that provides a novel way to fill paths. In Fact, the path don't have to be closed path. You can use the drawing Tool to Create intersecting lines, and convert your line work into a Live Paint group.

To start working with Live Paint, you first need to create some Intersecting lines using the Pencil, Pen, or Line Segment tool. The lines need to intersect because the Live Paint Bucket tool, which you'll use to color areas, needs to detect that an area Is closed(thatis,no gaps occur wherelines Intersect).Don't bother applying any complexappearances10 the lines (such as brushes,transparency,and variable stroke widths)because, as an alertwill warn you,those attributesarc lostwhen converting to a LivePaintgroup.

1 Using the Pencil tool ,', draw some Intersectinglines. Apply a stroke of 1 or 2 pts.

2 Select all of the path objects, and then do the following:

Select the live Paint Bucket tool (K), and click inside the selection.

A live Paint group is created and a color highlight appears along the border of the enclosed area that is under the pointer.

1 To fix the situation, choose View > Show Live Paint Gaps

If the Gaps are large, select the direct selection tool and drag the end point of one line across another line to close the gap.

Use Gap Options in a Live Paint Group

If you click with live Paint Bucket tool on a Selection of intersecting lines and nothing happens, you may have gaps where lines appear to intersect.

1 To fix this situation, choose View> show live Paint Gaps (if the option says Hide It's already done).

If the gaps are large, select the Direct Selection tool and drag the end Point of one line across another line to close the gap.

If the gaps are large, select the Direct Selection tool and drag the end Point of one line across another line to close the gap.

2 In the Gap Options dialouge box, Select Gap Detection and Preview.

3 Select an options from the Paint Stops At Menu

Short re Line indicators will appear across any gaps in the line work, significanting that Live paint feature now considers those areas be closed and able to be filled.

Expand or Release a Live Paint Group

You can not apply appearance attributes (such as brush strokes, transparency, and effects) to the individualfaces or edges of a Live Paintgroup.To apply these attributes, you need to expand or release the group intostandardIllustratorobjects.

A Live Paint group also needs to be expanded or released before you can export your artwork fileto a non-Adobe application.

1 Select a Live Paint group. Optionally, drag to create a copy of the group to preserve it for later use.

2 Do the following:

On the Control panel, click the Expand button to convert the separate paths in the Live Paint group intotwo nested groups of paths.

One group will contain standard filled path objects made from the former faces. The other group will containstandard path objects with strokes (andno fill) from theformer edges .

Add Gradient fill

A Gradient fill is a gradual blend between two or more solid colors. You can use gradients to add shading or volume in shape to create the appearance of depth in flat objects.

A gradient fill is composed of a strating and ending color. You can place additional solid colors between the strart and colors for more color variation in the fill. It spread from side to side across an object (Liner) or outward from the center of an object (radial).

Apply a gradient as a fill

1 To begin, select an object, then do the following:

Display the swatch panel, click the fill square on the panel, then click a swatch on the or on any open gradient library panel to apply it.

Apply a Gradient to a Stroke

In addition to applying a gradient to an object's fill, you can apply a gradient along or across an object's stroke.

To apply a gradient to a stroke:

1 Select an object. Apply a large stroke weightto better view the gradientyou are aboutto apply.

2 Do either of the following:

• Click the Stroke square on the main Gradient panel. Click the arrowhead next to the Gradient square to open the gradient menu, then select a gradienton the menu.

By default, the gradient will display within the stroke from left to right, with no attempt to follow the shape of the stroke.

4 Next , on the Gradient panel, click the Stroke square. click the Apply Gradient Along Stroke or apply Gradient Across Stroke icon.

Edit a Gradient via On Object controls

Sometimes, thebest way to editthe colorsandtheirexactposition ina gradientis after theoriginal gradient hasbeenapplied to an object.Working withthe interac• tive on-objectcontrols on thegradientannotatorenables you to immediately view your modifications.How cool isthat ?

To edita gradient on an object:

1On theGradientpanel, clickthe Fill square.

2Selectanobject, thenapplya gradient fill.

3 SelecttheGradienttool(G). The gradient annotator bar willdisplayon theobject. (If it doesn't, choose View> ShowGradient Annotator.)

4   Position   thepointerover   thebarto displaythecolorstops , thendo the following:

Double-click   a   stop   to   modify   the colorviathetemporarycolorpanel   you   learned about   earlier.ClickeithertheColoricon(for theColor panel controls)or theSwatches icon(for the Swatchespanel controls).

To modify a linear gradient with the annotator:

1Select anobject withalineargradient fill.

2Select the Gradient tool (G) The gradient annotator appeal's over the object.

3Do the following:

• To reposition wherethemiddle of the gradientfallswithin theobject,drag theround endpointin a perpendiculardirection to the colorbandsinthe gradient.

Modify a Radial Gradient via the Annotator

For a radial gradient, the gradient annotator displays a different set of editing controls. In this case, the controls enable you to modify the way gradient colorsspread from the centerto the edge of an object.

To modifya radialgradient withtheannotator:

1Select an object with a radial gradient fill.

2 Select the Gradienttool (G).The gradient annotator appears over the object.

3 Do the following:

• To reposition the gradient, drag either the bar or the larger of the two round endpoints.The center of the radial gradient does not need to remain centered on the object.

Chapter 7: Symbols

Symbols are perfect for creating repetitive designelements, suchas informationalicons for use on a map, or thegrass,flower,and tree shapes used ina landscape.

Symbols are more thanjust ready-madegraphics-they help create more efficientfiles. When you place multiplecopiesof a symbolin a file, Illustratordefines thesymbolobjectonly once inthe document code. This helpsreduce filestoragesize and speedsup bothprintoutputand down• loading times for web output. If you edit theoriginalsymbol,alloccurrences of thatsymbolinthedocumentwillupdateautomatic ally,saving you timeand effortinyour editing workflow.

Open Symbol Libraries

To Start working with symbols, you'll open and view some symbol libraries.

1 choose Window> symbols to display the Symbols Panel.

2 From the Symbol Libraries menu at the bottom of the symbols panel,select a library. A floatinng library panel opens.

3 Do the following :

click a symbol on the library panel to place it in the symbols panel.

Place a Single Symbol

In the Following steps, you'll place a single symbol, called an instance, in an Illustrator document. You will also see that an instance in your documents is linked to its symbols on the Symbols panel.

1 Display the Symbols panel

2 Do either of the following

Drag a symbol from the panel onto an artboard.

3 Place some other symbols in your document.

4 Click each instance in your document to see its matching symbols thumbail become selected on the symbols Panel. Note that the break link to Symbol icon also becomes highlighted,

veriyfing that the instance is linked to the symbols on the panel.

Place a set of Symbol

Here's where the fun starts with symbols. You'll use the Symbol Sprayer tool to spray multiple instances of a symbol and create a symbol set.

1 Select the Symbol Sprayer tool (or press Shift+S).

2 On the Symbols panel, click a symbol.

3 Click an artboard to spray one instance for each click or click and drag to quickly create multipleinstances. The instances will appear in a set within one bounding box.

Create Symbol

Oneor moreIllustrator objects can be madeinto a symbol.If you're planning to sprayyour custom symboldensely allover your artwork,try to avoidcreatingthe symbol from complex objectsto avoida performance slowdowninIllustrator,The objectfor your symbolcanbe anopenor closed path,a group, or type.It can containa brush strokeor effect.

1 Createone or moreobjects.Color andscale them as desired. Using the Selection tool~, Shift-click to selectall the objects.

2 On the bottomof the Symbolspanel,clickthe New Symbolicon

3 In the SymbolOptions dialogbox,entera name for the symbol.

4 Ifyour file willbe exportedto AdobeFlash, selectMovie Clip or Graphicfrom theExport 'typemenu. Ifthe symbolwillbe usedfor web output,selectAlign to PixelGridto preventblurry lineedges.

5Click OK.The symbolappearson theSymbols panel

To delete a symbol that is not used in the document, select it on the symbol panel. Click the delete symbol icon on the bottom of the symbols panel, then click Yes to confirm the deletion.

Edit a Symbol

You can easily edit a symbol that is either on the Symbol panel or placed as an instance in your document.

1 To edit a symbol, do either of the following

Double-click a symbol on the symbol panel. A temporary instance of the symbol will be placed in isolation mode.

2 Edit the object or objects

3 Press Esc to exit isolation mode. Any edits will be applied to the original symbol on the panel and to any instances that are linked to the symbol.

Symbol Shifter tool

The Symbol Shifter tool has two functions, The Tool shifts instances slightly in the direction you drag. shift-click to bring an instance in front of the others;

Option-shift-click (Mac Os) or Alt-shift-click (windows) to send an instances behind the others.

Symbol Scruncher Tool

The Symbol Scruncher tool affects the distance between instances. click and hold on a set to pull instances together. option+click (Mac Os) or Alt+click (windows) to push instances apart.

Symbol Sizer Tool

The Symbol Sizer tool scales instances by variable amounts. client an instance or drag across instances to enlarge some of them. Option- click or Alt+click (windows) to shrink instances.

Symbol Spinner Tool

Stainer Tool

The symbol stainer colorizes solid-color, pattern, and gradient fills contained in instances. Variable tints of the current fill color will be applied The lightness or darkness of the original color will be preserved.

Screener Tool

Save a Custom Symbol Library

Afteryou've created your ownuser-definedsymbolsand addedsymbols from some of thepredefined libraries to the Symbolspanel,youcan saveallof the symbolson thepanel to a custom library.

1 Create some custom symbols or edit some predefined symbols.

2 Add symbols from some of the predefined libraries to the Symbols panel.

3Onthebottomof the Symbolspanel,clickthe SymbolLibrariesmenuicon, thenselect Save Symbols from themenu.

4 Inthe SaveSymbolsAs Library dialog box, entera name,leavethelocation as theSymbolsfolder, thenclick Save.

Chapter 8: Pen & Pencil Tool

The Pentoolis one of the most powerfultools in theprogram.Itis also oneof themore difficulttools to learn. You use the tool to place anchor points and draw the straightor curvedsegmentsbetweenpoints. As you start to work with this tool, rememberthat you can always go back and tweak the pathshapeby moving points and readjusting curved segments-techniques that you have alreadylearned.

The Pencil tool enables you to draw in a freehandmanner to sketch a shape.The tool will createboththepoints and segmentson the freehand pathsyou draw.

The Pen tool creates precise curved and straight segments that are connected to anchor points. You can either click with the tool to create corner points and straight segments or drag with the tool to create smooth points and curved segments.

Straight-Sided Paths

The easier way to draw with the Pen tool is by clicking to create a straight-sided object.

1 Select the Pen tool (P) IP.

2 Make sure View> Smart Guides Is enabled to displaytemporary alignment guides while drawing.

3 Click to create the first anchor point. Reposition the pointer to place the second anchor point. The Rubber Band path preview option will visualize the next straight segment.

4 Click to create a second point and a straight segment.

5 click to create additional anchor points

6 To complete the shape, do the following

To complete the object as an open path and deselect it, command+click (Mac Os) or ctrl+click (Windows) away from the object, or press Esc.

Curved Path

When you drag the path tool, you will create an anchor point with smooth

curve and a pair of direction handles. If you rotate one direction handle for a smooth curve anchor point, the other handles move in tandem to preserve the smoothness of both curved segments attached to the point.

1 Select the Pen tool and make Sure that View > Smart Guides is enabled.

2 Drag to create the first anchor point. Two direction handles appear, aligned with the direction you drag. Release the mouse.

3 Position the tool pointer where you want the next point. the Rubber Band path preview option will visualize the next curved segment

4 To place the second anchor point, drag in the direction you want the curved segment to follow. the more you drag, the longer the direction handles you are creating will be.

5 Drag to create more anchor points and direction handles.

To complete the object as an path and deselect it, Command+click (Mac Os) or Ctrl+click (windows) away from the object or press Esc.

Convert Points

The points on a path can be converted from corner to curved or from curved to corner at any time. This features enables you to initially draw rough shapes composed of all corner points or all curved points, and then go back adjust individual points to create the desired path or shape. this is probably the most common way to create complex paths in illustrator.

Add or Remove Points

The Pen tool has yet another function: adding or removing points from a path. Below is a quick overview of these features.

To add a point to a selected path, roll the Pen tool over a segment, then click when the plus sign(+) indicatorappears by the pointer. (You could also click with the Add Anchor Point tool, located in the same tool group as the Pen tool.)Press A to select the Direct Selection tool, thendrag the new anchorpointto reshape the path.

To remove a selected point from a path, roll the Pen toolover the point,thenclick when the minus sign (-) indicator displays by the pointer.(You could also click with the Delete Anchor Point tool, located in the same tool group as the Pen tool, or click the RemoveSelectedAnchorPoints icon on the Controlpanel.)

Manually Trace a Raster Image

A common task in Illustrator is to use the Pen tool to manually trace the edges of a raster image to produce a clean,sharp-edgevector version of the image.Raster images are composed of pixelswith soft, subtle transitions between shapes inthe image.Raster images are good for reproducing continuous-tone photographs, but not good for producing sharp-edged artwork.

When tracing a raster image,placethe imageon its own top-level layer,thenuse the Transparency panel to lowerthe Opacity for the imageto 50%.Next, on the Layers panel, click the blank slot to the left of that layerlistingto lockit;this prevents objectson the layerfrom being selected.The lock icon appears in the slot. Click the lockiconto unlockthe layerand remove the icon.

After locking the raster image layer, use the Pen tool to create closed paths that followthe edges of colorareas in the image. Use the Eyedropper tool ~ (T) to sample colors from the areas inthe image, then apply those colorsto the path objectsyou have created.

Draw with the Pencil tool

ThePencil toolgives youthe chanceto showoffyourdrawingskills. You can drag thePenciltool t0createa freehand sketch consisting of open or closed paths.As withany path In Illustrator, you can go back laterand reshape segmentsand reposition points t0tweak your shape.

1Select the Pencil tool(N) ,'.

2Specify a stroke color and weight {width),and a fill color of None.

3 Draw lines. A preview line will follow your mouse movements. Release the mouse between strokes. that's all there is to it.

4To create a closed path with the Pencil tool, draw a path that returns to its starting point and release the mouse when a tiny circle indicater display by the tool painter.

Reshape Using the Pencil Tool

You can also use the Pencil tool to quickly reshape a portion any selected path, regardless of which tool or command was used to create the path.

1 Position the pencil tool over a portion of a selected open or closed path.

2 Drag to reshape the path

For an open path, you can finish up either on the path or off the path

For a closed path, you must finish up on another part of the path to avoid creating a new path insted.

Brushes Tool

Calligraphic : thin and thick contours on a path

scatter : shapes that are scattered on or around a path

Art : Graphic shapes or Image that are applied along a path

Bristle : Shades of color that mimic the bristle look of traditional art media

Pattern : A collection of graphic tiles that produce a stylish border or frame along the path.

Choose Window > Brushes to Display the Brushes panel.

click the Brush Libraries menu icon at the bottom of the panel, and select a library from a category submenu.

Edit Brushes

Illustrator offers specific options and settings that control the properties of each type of brush.

Edit a Calligraphic Brush

1 Select an object that has a calligraphic brush applied to its strokes.

2 on the Brushes panel, double-click the highlighted calligraphic brush thumbnail to edit it.

5Set theRoundness slider to alowvaluefor a narrow, thintipto createa thin andthick brushstroke, andkeep theSizevaluelow(youwilluse strokewidth to control brushsize).

6View your changes in the previewandon theselectedbrushstroke. Click OK, thenclick Apply to Strokes.

Edit an Art Brush

Options for an art brushfocuson how the graphic (art) object thatis usedinthe brushwillbe scaledon a path.

1Selectanobject that has an art brushappliedto its stroke .

2 On the Brushes panel, double-click thehighlighted artbrushthumbnail to editit.

3 In the Art Brush Options dialogbox, select Previewto sec your changes

4 Select a Brush Scale Option:

• Scale proportionately preserves the original proportions of the art object.

• Stretch To Ht Stroke Length allowsIllustrator to stretch (distort) the art objectto fit thepath.

•StretchBetweenGuidesallowsyou to movethedashedguidesinthe previewto define whichpartof theartobject Illustrator can stretchand which partwillbe preserved(not stretched).

5 View your changes on the selected brush stroke. ClickOK,thenclickApply to Strokes.

Edit a PatternBrush

A patternbrush is composed of up to five tiles,each placedon a specificpart of a path (outercorner,innercorner, side,start, or end).Editingthe brushinvolves choosingimageryfor each tileand determining how the tilesare scaledon a path.

2 Apply the patternbrush you want to editto an object, and keep the object selected.

3 On the Brushespanel,double-click the highlighted patternbrush thumbnail to editit.

The PatternBrushOptions dialog box displaysfivetilethumbnails,each with a menuand a diagram of where that tile will be used on a path.

4Clicka tile thumbnail, then choose one of your new patternswatches from the menu.Do this for each substitutetile part you created

5 Click a Fit option to determine how the pattern is adjusted to fit a path.

6 view your changes in the preview area at lower left.

Create a Watercolor Wash Effect

You can use watercolor brushes (accessed from the Artistic Watercolor brush library) to paint strokes of different color tints on a separate layer stacked behind a line art sketch.

You can paint using colors from the swatches panel or you can use the Eyedropper tool to sample a color from any placed photographic image, then paint with the sampled color. consider saving the sampled color as a swatch.

Chapter 9: Type Tool

You can create a decorative type that functions as a graphic or a headline and create body type for reports, brochure, and product pieces.

Create Text Type

Text type Stands by itself and is not associated with any drawn path or object. It can be composed of just one character or a group of several words, and it is most suitable for headlines, titles, or lables for web buttons.

1 Display the character panel by choosing Window > Type > character.

2 Choose View > Show Bounding Box.

3 Select Type Tool (T). Click a Blank area of an artboard. A flashing text insertion point appears.

4 Do the following

On the control panel, select a point size from the font Size menu.

5 select a fill color and a stroke of None .

6 Enter some type. To complete the type object, do either of the following

Press Esc to automatically switch to the selection tool.

Style point Type

After entering type, you can use the Character, color, Swatches, or Appearance panel to apply different styles (fonts, size, spacing), color or effects to a selected type object. the type will remain editable

To style point type:

1 Select the point type by clicking on it using either selection tool.

2 To resize the type, do either of the following on the character panel, change the Font Size value or choose a preset size from the menu.

3 To change the font, click the Font Family menu arrow to display the list of available fonts in your system.

4 Roll over a font listing, then press the up Arrow or Down Arrow key to preview different

font families on the selected type. Press Return (Mac os) or Enter (Windows) to apply the highlighted font.

5 To change the font style (weight or slant of the character face), choose a listing from the Font Style menu.

6To modify the spacingbetween allthe characters in the type object,change the valueinthe Trackingfield, choose a preset valuefrom the menu, or hold down Command-Option (Mac OS) or Ctrl-Alt (Windows) and press the Right Arrow or Left Arrow key.Positive valuesincrease (loosen) the spacing;negative values reduce (tighten)the spacing.

7To modify the spacing between twocharacters,click withtheType tool betweentwocharacters, thenchange the valuein the Kerningfield or hold downOption (Mac OS) or Alt(Windows)andpressthe RightArrowor Left Arrowkey.Positive values increasethe spacing; negative values reduce the spacing.

Apply Effect to Type

Youcan apply aneffect from the Effectmenu orfromthe AddNew Effectmenu on theAppearance panelto a selected type object .

An effect can be removed at anytime viathe Appearance panel.

Wrap Text

To wraptext aroundart:

1 Positionan art objector symbolin frontof the text rectangle.

2 Selectbothobjects,thenchooseObject> Text Wrap > Make. Text in the rectangleflows aroundthe art object'sedge.

3To adjustthe distance betweenthe edge of the art objectandthe text, choose

Object> Text Wrap > Text Wrap Options.

4In the Text Wrap Optionsdialog box, select Preview, thenincreasethe Offset valueto increasethe space aroundthe art object. Press Tab to preview any new values.Click OK.

Reposition Type on a Path

Once placed on a path, thetypecanbe repositioned along orflippedto the opposite sideof thepath.

To change the position of type on a path:

1Using the Selection tool, click the type path'sobject. Center, left, andrightcontrol brackets appear.

2 To repositionthetypeblock, do anyof thefollowing:

•To move thetypeblock along thepath, dragthecenter bracketright or left

Flow Type on Circle

To position type on a circle:

1 Createa circle, then use the Scissors tool ~to cuttwoopposite anchor points onthepath.

2 Using the Type On A Path tool "< (, enter type firston the upper semi-circular object,then on the lowersemi-circular object

3 Adjust the position of the type on each selected path object by dragging their

respective center brackets. Use the Baseline Shift option on the character panel to shift the type above or below its path.

4 Place other objects in front or behind the type objects to enhance the logo.

Create Outline Type

When you are finished editing and styling type, you can convert the type into outlines. The converted "graphic" objects will no longer be editable type, but the characters paths can be reshaped and transformed using all the editing techniques.

1 Create a large point type object, then choose Type > Create Outlines to convert the type to individual objects.

2 Using the direct Selection tool, drag any point, segment, or direction handle to modify the shape of the path.

3 Reposition or transform any of the objects and apply a different fill or stroke color to some or all of the objects.

Chapter 10: Advanced Drawing

Illustrator isn't limited to working with vector object only. Bitmap images can be incorporated into your artwork as imagery that is placed either next to behind vector objects or that is used as a fill within an object.

To place an embedded image:

1ChooseFile> Place.In the Place dialog box, locate and select one or more Images.

2 Deselect Link at the bottom of the dialog box.

3 If the image is from Photoshop and contains multiplelayers, selectShow ImportOptions.ClickPlace.

4 In the PhotoshopImportOptionsdialogbox, do eitherof the following:

Click Convert Layers 'lbObjects to preserve each layer as a nested object within a group on the Layers panel.Transparencyvaluesare listed as editableappearances on the Appearance panel. Blendingmodes that are also available In Illustrator are preserved and remaineditable.(For a list of blending modes in

Illusrrator, view the BlendingModes menu on the Transparency panel.)

Click Flatten Layers To A Single Image to create a flattened version of the file.

5 Click OK.

The loaded graphics Icon appears. The icon displays a thumbnail of the first loadedImage and lists the total number of loaded Images.

6Press the Left Arrow or RightArrow key to cycle throughthe thumbnailson the loaded graphics icon. Drag to place an image.Drag again to place the next loaded Image.

Place Bitmap Images as Link

You can also choose to place a linked image into your document. Illustrator places a screen version of the Image to serve as a placeholder and maintains a link to the external source file.

Use the Control Panel

The Left side of the Control panel displays the name of a selected linked image, its color mode and its ppi value.

The Control panel also enables you to manage a linked image by providing access to the same controls found on the inks panel;

Click the linked image file name to display a menu containing the same options as found on the links panel.

Create Clipping Mask

When objects are part of a clipping mask, the top mostobjectcrops (masks)the objects that are belowit. Portions of the lower objectsthat fall withinthe path of the topmostobject remain visible,while portionsthat extend beyond its path are hiddenand don'tprint.

To create a clipping mask:

1 Arrange one or more objects to be masked on an artboard. Stackthe object that will become the maskin front of the otherobjects.

Select all of the objects.

2Choose Object> Clipping Mask > Make.The objectswill be masked by the topmostobject .

On the Layers panel, a new Clip Group appearsthat containsthe objects in the clipping mask.The topmostobjectin the groupwillbe convertedinto a ClippingPath and be listedas such on the Layers panel.

Use Image Trace

a simplified version composedof a limited set of colors,shades, or just line work. You can apply Image Trace t.o a linked or embeddedimagethat.you've placed into your document.Use the Image Trace panelt.o access all the optionsfor this feature.

To trace an image:

1 Select a placedimage.Choose Window > Image Trace to displaythe panel.

2 Click one of the six tracing preseticons alongthe top of the panel or select an optionfrom the Preset menu. A series of progress bars will appear and a tracing will be generated.

3 From the view menu on the image Trace panel, select an option to view the resulting paths. The default setting is Tracing Result.

Expand a Tracing

To expand a training, select a tracing object, then click Expand on the Control panel. The former Layers panel listing of Image Tracing will be converted into a Group listing, with the path objects nested within the group.

ArtBrush

Experimentwith applyinga logo as an art brush.Selectthe logo objector group. Click New Brush on the Brushes paneland select Art Brush to convertthe object intoan art brush.Use the Paintbrushtool to draw a stroke withthe new art brush across a curved shapeinthe drawing.

3DMapping

To experiment with 3D mapping, drag the artwork logo that you want to fit onto a 3D shape into the Symbolspanelto create a new symbol. To create a sphere, draw a curved path shape, apply a white stroke, then chooseEffect

> 3D > Revolve.In the 3D Revolve Options dialog box, under Revolve, select From:Left Edge, then click Map Art. In the Map Art dialog box, select your new symbolfrom the Symbol menu.Drag the symbol in the light/shadow preview to position it on the sphere. Click OK twice.

14. Output

Now thatyou havecreated variousartworkpieces in Illustrator,it'stime to focuson outputting high-qualityfiles, whetheritbefor printor web. Preparing an artworkfile for its destinationformatrequires performing a number of tasks.

For print, these tasks involve confirmingthatcolors are defined correctly as process or spot,previewing colorseparations, and specifying appropriate settingsinthePrint dialog box.For web and screen, these tasks involve specifying thecorrectcolormode,andaligningobject pathsto thepixel grid. Both typesof output requirechoosinga resolution for certaineffectsthatwillberasterized whentheartworkisexported.

In this chapter, you will learnwhattheessential settings areinthePrint dialog box,andhow toexport anIllustrator file tothe JPEG,PNG,andSVG formats.

Prepare Artwork for Web Output

Web and screen output have their own requiremnts that need to be addressed to ensured quality output.

Document color Mode

web browsers and mobile screens display images in RGB color

Choose File > Document color Mode > RGB color.

Artboard Size

Selectthe Artboard toolto enterArtboardmode.Resizethe artboardsto matchthe pixeldimensions of the web pages you are exportingto. Ask your web developerfor these dimensions.

Align to Pixel Grid

Whenand Illustrator fileisexportedto eitherthe JPEG or PNG format, the artwork will be rasterized, meaningvector pathsand shapeswill be convertedto pixels and lose their crisp, sharpedges.

To minimize blurring along edges, Illustratorprovides the Align to Pixel Grid feature.This feature automatically positions any vertical and horizontal path segment on an object to align with the pixel grid, even if the object is moved or scaled. (Path segments that are not vertical or horizontal are not aligned.)

To align all future object, do either of the following :

For a New Document, choose File>New to open the New Document dialouge box. Select Web from the Profile menu. Align New Object to Pixel Grid is selected automatically.

Pixel Preview

The Pixel Preview feature enables you to see how exported web artwork will appear. With either Align To Pixel Grid optionactive,choose View > Pixel Preview to pre view the artwork as a 72 ppi (pixels per inch) bitmapimage. Vertical and horizontal paths thatare aligned to the grid will not appear blurry.

Resolution for Rasterized Effects

Since web and screen displaysare oftensmall devices with low-resolutionoutput(comparedto printoutput),a lower resolutionsettingcan be appliedto any raster effects.

The stepsfor using the DocumentRaster Effects Settings dialog box are the same as in the "Prepare Artwork for Print Output"sectionearlier in this chapter,except you would choose Screen (72 ppi) from the Resolutionmenu.

Export Art work

Illustratorprovides ways to exportfiles to JPEG or PNG format(two of the most popularformatsused for web imagery)and also to SVG format(a format gaining in popularitybecause it preserves vectorpathsand shapes in the exported graphicsfile).

Export to JPEG or PNG Format

The JPEG and PNG file formats describe an image as a grid of pixels and generate a file thatis compact,but set to a specific resolution.

To export artwork in JPEG or PNG format:

1 Choose File > Export.

2In the Export dialog box, select a location for the file

3From the Format (Mac OS) or Save As Type (Windows) menu, select either PNG or JPEG. Select Use Artboards, then click All or entera Range value.

4ClickExport. The JPEGor PNG Options dialogbox willopen.

• In the JPEG Options dialog box, set the Quality slider to between5 and7.

• In the PNG Options dialog box from the Resolution menu, select Screen (72 ppi).From the Background Color menu, select Transparent.

5Click OK to exportthe file to the preferredformat.

Export SVG

SVGis a vector formatthatdescribes images as shapes,paths,and optimized effects. SVG files are small and display as sharp-edged shapes on the web and on mobile devices. SVG shapes can be scaled onscreen withoutany loss to theirclear, sharp edges.

1 ChooseFile>Save As.In the Save As dialog box, select a location.

2 Fromthe Format (Mac OS) or Save As Type (Windows)menu, selectSVG. Select Use Artboards, then clickAll or enter a Range value.

4From the SVG Profiles menu, select SVG 1.1. Leave the Type menu set to SVG.

5If the Illustrator file contains any linked placed images, selectEmbedfrom the Image Locationmenu.This will make the images part of the SVG file.

6Click OK to exportthe file to SVG format.

Prepare Artwork for Print Output

In Illustrator, getting the high-qualitygraphicsto outputsatisfactorily requires more work.

Illustratorvector objectsare resolution independent. They will printat theresolution of the printingdevice. The higher the device resolution, the higher the edge quality of shapes in the printedimage.

Document Color Mode

Whenyou'repreparinga filefor print,you firstneed to know whattype of printer willbe used.

COMMERCIALPRESS: CMYKCOLOR

A commercial press printscolorsin the artworkas process colorswhich are a combinationof the four CMYK inkcolors. Eachink coloris printed separately onto a roll of paper usingoneof four colorplates-a Cyan, Magenta,Yellow,andBlack plate. Forthistype of printer, make suretheFile>Document ColorMode submenu is set to CMYK Color.Commercial printing is used when dozens (if not hundreds) of copies of the file are needed.

COMPOSITE COLOR PRINTER: RGB COLOR

A composite colorprinterprints allthe colorstogether directlyon a single sheetof paper.Forthistype of printer, make suretheFile>DocumentColor Modesubmenu is setto RGBColor.The printerwillconvertthe Illustratorfile from RGBColor modeto CMYK Colormodeand willproduce aprintusingthefourCMYK color inks.Use composite printerswhen you need onlyonecopy (or afew) of thefile.

Art board Size

Hereare someguidelinesfor artboardsizein regard to print output.

• Whenprintingto acompositeprinter,makesure the sizeof eachartboardis lessthanor equal to thesize of the printermedia(thepaper).

• Whenprinting to a commercial printer,makesurethesizeof eachartboard is lessthanthesizeof theprinter mediaso thatanyprinter's marks will display

• If you need to scalethe artboardand artworkdown to fit the printmedia, see the informationaboutthe Scalingmenuin the "Print Dialog Box Settings" section laterin thischapter.

Bleed

For eitherprintertype, make sure objects that need to printrightto the edge of the paper extend off the edge of the artboardslightly.The part of an object thatis beyond the edge is referred to as a bleed.

Resolution forRasterized Effects

Raster (bltrnapped) effects are effects that will be applied as pixels and not as vector shapes.Raster effects include SVGfilters;Drop Shadow,Inner andOuterGlows,and the Feather commands from the Effect>Sryllzesubmenu alongwith allPhotoshop Effects listed inthe Effect menu.

To determine the resolution that will be applied to raster effects:

1ChooseEffect>Document   RasterEffects Settings.

2IntheDocument RasterEffects Settingsdialogbox, select High (300 ppi)[pixelsper inch] from the Resolution menu .

3UnderBackground,clickTransparent.

4 Click OK.Settings will be applied to any raster effects in the document.

Chapter 11: Getting To Know The Work Area

Opening an Illustrator file

You may be in charge of marketing efforts in your firm but are not a designer; you may or may not have purchased the Adobe application.

Because graphic design is a constant process in marketing, you may be required to review Illustrator files from vendors, partners, and designers. Have an exciting feel of the new Illustrator 2022 by going through the steps below;

Click twice on the Adobe Illustrator icon to

open the Adobe Illustrator.

Click on File > click on the Open button on the home screen > click Open in order to open the design.

Select Window > Workspace >Essentials, ensure it is selected then click on Window > Workspace > Reset Essentials to rest the workspace.

Click on the View option > Fit Artboard in Window.

To gain access to your files anywhere and at any time, it is best to save your document as cloud documents.

This way it will be saved to the Adobe Creative Cloud. To do this;

Click on File > Save As. Then click on the option to save to the Creative Cloud button.

Any time you have a need to work on a cloud document simply;

Click on File > Open. In the Open dialog box, click on Open Cloud Document, you can then open a cloud document from the dialog box that is displayed.

Whenever you open Illustrator, you can choose your Files from the Home screen in order to see documents you have saved to the Creative Cloud you can then open and arrange.

Exploring the workspace

You can choose to design and organize your documents and files with the use of different elements like panels, bars, and windows. The arrangement of elements such as these is known as a workspace. The workspaces of the various applications that are in Creative Cloud look alike hence moving between different applications can be quite easy. Illustrators can be adapted to your mode of work by choosing various preset workspaces or by creating one of your own.

The application bar in the workspace located across the top by default contains application controls, the workspace switcher, and search. On Windows, the main menu bar items display in in line with the Application bar.

Panels are used in monitoring and modifying your work. Various panels are shown by default in the panel dock on the right side of the workspace, and any panel can be shown by simply choosing it from the Window menu.

The toolbar contains various tools that are used in designing and also editing artwork, artboard, and also editing images. Tools that work in the same way are usually grouped together.

The status bar is usually located on the lower left side of the Document window. It shows information, zooming, and navigation controls.

Finally, the Document window shows the files you are currently working on.

Getting to know the toolbar

The Fill and Stroke boxes, drawing modes, and screen modes are all found in the toolbar on the left side of the workspace, along with tools for selecting, drawing, painting, editing, and viewing. You'll learn about the exact functions of many of these tools as you progress through the sessions.

Drag the pointer over the Selection tool located in the toolbar.

Drag the pointer over the Direct Selection tool then tap and hold until a tool menu is displayed you can then let go of the mouse button.

Select the Group Selection tool in the menu to choose it. Note that any tool that is in the toolbar and shows a small triangle has some additional tools that can be chosen in this same method.

Click and hold down the Rectangle tool to show more tools. Click on the arrow located on the right side of the hidden tools panel in order to separate the tools from the toolbar as a different floating panel of tools that can be accessed with ease.

Select the close button which is the X icon at the upper corner of the floating tool (windows) or the upper left corner (macOS). The tools will then go back to the toolbar.

Finding more tools

The default collection of tools in Illustrator's toolbar does not include all of the available tools. As you progress through this book, you'll learn about other tools that you'll need to know how to use. The section below shows how these other tools can be accessed whenever you have a need for them.

Select the Edit Toolbar option at the lower part of the toolbar. A panel will then display a list of all the available tools. Dimmed tools are those that are already in the default toolbar.

Drag the pointer over a tool that is dimmed, like the selection tool at the top of the tools list.

Move through the list of tools until you can see the Shaper tool. If you would like to add the tool, move the shaper tool to the Rectangle tool. When you notice a high light around the rectangle tool, let go of the mouse button in order to include the shaper tool.

Note that you can make use of the same method described above to choose any other tool you would like to make use of.

Working with the Properties panel

In Illustrator, the Properties panel displays settings and controls in the context of your current task or workflow. This new panel was created with simplicity in mind, ensuring that you have quick access to the controls you require.

In the Essentials workspaces, the Properties panel is enabled by default. You may also view it by going to

Window > Properties.

Working with panels

Many of the tools and choices that make editing artwork easier are accessible through panels like the Properties panel. The Window menu in Illustrator lists all of the panels available alphabetically. After that, you'll try hiding, opening, and closing panels.

Hide or show all panels

To hide or display panels which also include the toolbar and the control panel simply press the Tab button.

To hide or display all panels with the exception of the toolbar and the control panel, tap the Shit + Tab buttons.

Moving and docking panels

Panels in Illustrator can be rearranged and structured in the workspace to suit your needs. Then, on the right side of the workspace, you'll open a new panel and dock it with the default panels.

Select the Window menu at the top of the screen to view all of the panels that can be found in Illustrator. Select Align from the Window menu in order to open the Align panel and some other panels grouped with it by default.

Move the Align panel group close to the title bar located at the top of the panel names to move the group closer to the docked panels on the right.

Move the Align panel close to the panel tab on the Properties, Layers, and Libraries panels tabs on the right.

Click on the X icon at the top of the Transform and Pathfinder panel group which is free-floating in order to have it closed.

Move the Align panel close to the panel tab to the left side far from the dock of panels then let go of the mouse button.

Select the X icon at the top of the Align panel in order to close it.

Switching workspaces

You can also choose to alter components of the default Essentials workspace, like the toolbar and panels, as you've seen. You can keep that particular arrangement as a workspace and move between them while working as you make modifications, such as opening and closing panels and adjusting their position.

After that, you'll transfer workspaces and become acquainted with some new panels.

Click on the workspace option on the right end of the Application bar located at the top of the docked panels in order to change the workspace. Various workspaces will be listed with what they do that will open panels and also arrange the workspace accordingly.

Select the Layout option from the workspace switcher menu in order to make changes to the workspaces.

Click on Essentials from the workspace switcher at the top of the docked panels to change back to the Essentials workspace.

Click on the Reset Essentials option from the workspace switcher in the Application bar. When you return to the previous workspace, it will recall any changes you must have made such as choosing the library panel.

Saving a workspace

After you've set up your panels and tools to your preference, save your workspace.

Choose Window > Workspace > New Workspace... from the menu and give it a name. In your new workspace, all of your tools and panels are saved in their current state. From the same menu, you may switch between workspaces.

Illustrator automatically saves changes to the active workspace as you move tools and panels while working.

By selecting Window > Workspace > Reset, you can restore a workspace to its prior condition (workspace name).

Using panel and context menus

When you click on the panel menu icon in Illustrator you will find more panels that have some additional options that can be used to alter the panel display, add or alter panel content, and lots more. Follow the sets of instructions below to make changes to the display of the Swatches panel with the use of the panel menu.

With the use of the Selection tool that must have been chosen in the toolbar on the left side then click on the bowl shape again.

Choose the Fill color box to the left side of the word Fill in the Properties panel.

In the panel that displays, ensure that the Swatches option is chosen toward the top of the panel.

Click the panel menu icon in the upper-right corner and choose small list View from the panel menu.

Choose the same panel menu icon in the panel that is displaying then select Small Thumbnail View to return the Swatches to their original view.

Click on the Escape to hide the swatches panel.

Click on Select > Deselect so that the bowl shape will no longer be selected.

Drag the pointer over the dark gray area which surrounds the artwork. You can then right-click to display the context menu with the specific option.

Changing the view of the artwork

Adobe Illustrator's default view is for all artwork to be previewed in color. You can, however, choose to simply see the artwork's outlines (or paths) when you display it. When working with intricate artwork, viewing it without paint characteristics reduces the time it takes to redraw the screen.

Linked files are presented as outlined boxes with an X within in Outline mode by default. Select Show Images in Outline Mode from File > Document Setup to see the contents of connected files.

On screens with a resolution greater than 2000 pixels in width or height, you can examine your artwork as outlines in Illustrator's GPU Preview mode. When viewing artwork in GPU Outline mode, the paths are smoother and the time it takes to redraw complicated artwork on high-density display screens is reduced.

If you would like to view all artworks as outlines, click on view > Outline or press the Ctrl + E for windows or command + E for macOS. Select view > Preview to go back to previewing artwork in color.

If you would like to view all artwork in a layer as outlines, press the Ctrl button and then click on the eye symbol for the layer in the layers panel.

Take note that the eye icon will have a hollow center when the Outline view is enabled and a filled center when you enable the preview view.

Using view commands

View commands are used to have the view of the artwork reduced or enlarged with ease and they can be found in the view menu.

Click on the view option then Zoom In twice in order to make the display of the artwork bigger. Note that when you make use of the viewing tools and the command it only affects the display of the artwork and not the size of the artwork.

Click on View > Fit Artboard in Window for you to see the whole artwork again.

Using the Zoom tool

Want to be able to freely zoom in and out while working on a specific portion of your design? In fact, you must always zoom in and out to inspect and alter your design. It's nearly impossible to complete a design without zooming in. By clicking on your Artboard, you may swiftly zoom in and out with the zoom tool.

To utilize the zoom tool, press Z on the keyboard. As an alternative, you can also choose to click on the Edit Toolbar option and then click on Navigate > Zoom Tool.

You have the option of using a single or double click. You can zoom in on a smaller scale with a single click, and you can zoom out twice the size of your present work area with a double click.

Panning in a document

You may generate video-like effects from pictures or movie clips by using the pan and zoom tool in Adobe Premiere Elements. When it comes to video clips, the effect works best when the objects in the clip move very little.

You pick objects and the order in which they are panned and zoomed into when working with the pan and zoom tool. You can customize the effect in Adobe Premiere Elements to meet your specific needs.

Panning with the Navigator panel

The Navigator Panel eliminates the inconvenience of continual zooming in and out. By clicking on within the panel, the currently active region (shown as a red rectangle) can also be altered. The currently viewed region in the illustration window is represented by the colored box in the Navigator (also known as the proxy view area).

Navigate to Windows -> Navigator to display the panel. The artwork is displayed in the Navigator panel's thumbnail view in the figure below.

Viewing artwork

The current Illustrator document's active artboard takes up the entire screen in Presentation mode. The application's menu, panels, guidelines, grids, and all available options are hidden in this mode. Only the artwork from the artboard is shown in this non-editable mode. For displaying design concepts, this method is effective.

One of the following actions will put you in presentation mode:

Click on View > presentation mode.

Press the Shift + F buttons.

Navigating multiple artboards

Pressing the left or right arrow keys will take you to the previous or next artboard, respectively, when navigating between the artboards. To switch to the following artboard, click anyplace else.

Press the Esc key to exit this mode.

Rotating the view

You can easily design your logos, packaging, page layouts, typography, and other graphics by rotating the canvas with the Rotate view function.

The specified angle is applied to all of your artboards and other visible items. After that, you can carry on working as you normally would in the standard view.

If you would like to rotate the view with the use of the Rotate View tool, follow the instructions below;

Select and hold the hand tool and then click on the Rotate View tool.

Move the Rotate View tool anywhere on the canvas in order to alter the orientation of the canvas.

If you would like to navigate between various angles, make use of the widget that is displayed when you rotate the canvas view.

Drag anywhere on the canvas to rotate the canvas view. Press and hold Space+Shift to switch from the currently chosen tool to the Rotate View tool.

Chapter 12: Techniques For Selecting Artwork

Starting the lesson

In this lesson, I will introduce you to the fundamentals of creating, editing, and selecting with the use of Illustrator as they are the building blocks of most designs you might be working on.

Selecting objects

The Selection tool is one of the most fundamental and critical tools that you should understand first. Simple but effective You must first pick the objects before applying any effects or adding color. Your workflow will go more quickly if you choose many objects to which you'll apply the same style and effect.

To select a tool simply;

Click on the Selection Tool (V) from the toolbar then select and move the object you would like to select.

When an object is selected, its layer colors will be used to highlight it. If there are things in between that you don't want to choose, holding the Shift key and clicking on the objects you want to select is a better option. Alternately, you can

Click and drag to choose, then deselect, the intervening undesired objects.

Using the selection tool

In Illustrator, you can choose an object in a number of ways. You can choose an object's stroke or fill it with the Selection tool. Only when the path is shown in Preview mode and the Object Selection by Path Only check box is deselected in the Selection & Anchor Display options can you choose an object using the fill.

You can add or remove items from your selection after you've already chosen one or more. Additionally, you can choose specific areas of the object by dragging a marquee with the Selection tool, or you can drag over a specific area to make a selection rectangle.

Selecting and editing with the Direct Selection tool

You can choose, move, or alter particular points or path segments in a path or a form with the Direct Selection tool.

Select the Direct Selection tool.

Choose the object so you can see its anchor points and path segments.

Click an anchor to select it or you can also choose to click on the Shift + Click to choose the select multiple anchor points, path segments, or both.

Move the anchor point, handle, or path segment in order to alter the shape or object.

Selecting with the use of a marquee

The marquee selection tool may be found in the Illustrator menu's Tools panel. The rectangle that is drawn with the marquee selects everything that is touched or bound by it. Only pixels are selectable when using Illustrator, much like Photoshop. In Illustrator, there are no genuine pixels, only objects. Text, drawn shapes, imported art, and embedded raster (i.e., bitmap) images are all examples of objects. However, unlike Photoshop, Illustrator does not allow you to choose a portion of a bitmap. Only the object can be chosen or ignored.

It is possible to pick pathways (such as a circle) as well as the specific points or sections that make up those paths. This enables you to move, rotate, resize, or delete a portion of a path. The object is still selected, so any changes to the fill or stroke color will apply to the entire object, not just the areas that have been chosen.

Hiding and locking objects

When working on a particular detail of a particular area of a layer, you may not always want to lock the entire layer. You can lock the completed items while continuing to work on the others.

Choose the objects you want to lock and then navigate to the overhead menu, Object >Lock > Selection.

To hide objects,

Click on the object you wish to hide then click on hide.

All these will be done in the Swatches panel. By clicking the eye icon, a layer can be hidden or turned off. Simply click on the box whenever you wish to make a layer visible again, and the eye icon will reappear to indicate that the layer is active.

Unlocking objects

Do you want to make changes to the locked layer? Easy. In order to unlock,

Click the lock icon.

A different approach is to select Object > Unlock All.

Selecting similar objects

You can choose artwork with the

Select > Same command based on similar fill color, stroke color, stroke weight, and more. An object's border or contour is its stroke, and its breadth is its stroke weight.

Selecting in Outline mode

All artwork is displayed in Adobe Illustrator by default with the paint elements fill and stroke (border) visible. The appearance of the artwork is eliminated when you view it in outline mode, leaving just the outlines (or paths), which are visible.

Click on View > Outline in order to see the artwork as an outline.

To select in the outline mode,

Click on the edge of the object or move a marquee across the shape to choose it. Furthermore, some of the forms may have a little X in their center while you are in Outline mode. You can choose the shape by clicking that X.

Aligning objects

When constructing layouts, text, and logos, it's crucial to align your elements. Spend around two minutes selecting the graphic (object) and text,

choosing Vertical Align Center, then repeating this for the remaining two to make it look more professional. Select all text then choose Left-Hand Horizontal Alignment.

The final step is to select all graphics and then horizontally align them from left to center.

Aligning objects to each other

A grouped object can be aligned, but other objects in the same group won't move about within the group.

A grouped item, for instance, will move further to the left of the Artboard if you align it to the left.

You must first ungroup the objects in order to align them, then group them back together if you want to align a specific portion of a grouped object to the left.

Aligning to a key object

You can decide which object to align with the others. This object will be the key object.

Choose the objects you would like to align to the key object then click on the Align To >show options > Align to Key Object.

Distributing objects

Use the distribute spacing option to spread objects uniformly.

Choose Align to Key Object from the drop-down box if you need a precise measurement of the distance between your objects. Before pressing the distribute spacing button, enter the size (vertical or horizontal depending on the orientation you want).

Aligning anchor points

Select the Direct-Selection tool, hold down Shift, and click on the anchor points you would like to align or distribute. Note that the last anchor points you select becomes the key anchor point. The Align to Key Anchor option is automatically selected in the Align panel and Control panel.

In the Align panel or Control panel, select the button for the type of alignment or distribution you want.

Aligning to the artboard

Click on the objects you would like to align or distribute.

With the use of the Selection tool, Shift-click on the artboard you want to use to activate it. The active artboard has a darker outline than the others.

In the Align panel or Control panel, choose Align to Artboard and then select the button for the type of alignment or distribution you want.

Working with groups

Objects can be grouped together to function as a single entity. In this approach, you can change or transfer a group of items without changing any of their unique properties or how they relate to one another. Additionally, it can make picking out paintings simpler.

Grouping items

You can group together numerous items so that they are handled as a single entity. Then, you can change or transfer a variety of things without changing their properties or nearby placements. For instance, grouping the elements in a logo design will allow you to resize and move it as a single object.

The grouping may alter the layering of objects and their stacking order on a particular layer since grouped objects are placed sequentially on the same layer of the artwork and after the frontmost object in the group. Objects are grouped in the layer of the topmost selected object when you pick several objects in different layers and then group them.

Choose the objects that should be grouped.

Editing a group in Isolation mode

Isolation Mode in Adobe Illustrator is frequently used to edit specific items within groups or sub-layers. When you are working in isolation mode, everything that isn't selected will dim out to help you concentrate.

You can separate the items from their groups for editing and then reassemble them, but using isolation mode is simply quicker and more effective, especially if you have numerous sublayers or groups. Multiple groups ungrouping may cause the subgroups to become messed up, although isolation mode wouldn't.

If you want to alter an item or set of objects, you can do so by right-clicking, double-clicking, using the Layers panel, or the Control Panel.

Creating a nested group

In order to create larger groups, groups can be nested, or grouped inside of other objects or groups. In the Layers panel, groups are represented as Group> elements. To add and remove objects from groups, use the Layers panel.

Click on either object > Group or Object.

Exploring object arrangement

As you create them, Illustrator layers each object on top of the previous one, starting with the first one. The stacking order of the objects impacts how they appear when they overlap. Using the Layers panel or the Arrange commands, you may always change the order in which the objects in your artwork are stacked.

Arranging objects

Make use of the Selection tool then click on the object option that can be found at the top of the artboard on the left-hand side.

Click on the Arrange button located in the Properties panel. Select the Send to Back in order to send the shape to the back of all of the other shapes.

Click on the Arrange button again then click on Bring Forward as many times as possible in order to bring the black shape mentioned above.

The above must nuggets must have been enlightening, now I am sure you know how to use the selection tool, hide and unlock objects when you have the need to, align objects which also includes aligning to key objects and aligning to artboards, and also the grouping of items. I want to be sure you have a perfect understanding of the above-discussed points and to that effect, you should take the activity below.

Ensure you answer all of the questions without having to look at the points above to get answers. You can read the chapter again and again for perfect understanding before answering the questions.

Activity

1.What is a selection tool?

2.How do you select and edit objects in illustrator?

3.What are the steps to follow to have objects hidden?

4.What is an Outline mode?

5.Why should objects be aligned?

6.Draw a square and mark out its anchor points?

7.What is the importance of grouping items? Group a rectangle, a square, and a circle together while indicating their anchor points.

8.What are the steps taken to have objects arranged?

Chapter 13: Using Shapes To Create Artwork For A Postcard

Shapes are very important when it comes to working with Illustrator and creating artwork. This lesson will further enlighten you on the creation of documents, the shapes you can make use of, and also how you can make changes to shapes.

Starting the lesson

In this lesson, you will learn how to create shapes and also how you can edit shapes with ease. Start your Adobe Illustrator to get started.

Creating a new document

Before arts can be added you have to begin with creating a new document. Follow the steps below to create new documents;

To start a new document, select File > New.

On the right side of the dialog box locate the Preset Details area and then insert a name for the document. Note the name you insert now will also be the name of the Illustrator file when you save it.

To start a new document, click Create.

Select Save As under File. Click Save On Your Computer to save the document locally if the Cloud Document dialog box appears.

Working with basic shapes

You'll design a number of fundamental shapes in the first section of this class, including rectangles and polygons.

Since the endpoints of the path are joined, a shape is referred to as a closed path. Your shapes are made up of anchor points and the pathways that connect them. As a line, a path can also be open. Endpoints are the distinct anchor points at either end of an open path.

Creating rectangles

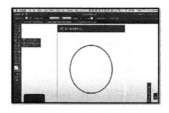

Set your fill and stroke colors in the Properties panel before selecting the Rectangle tool.

Create a rectangle by dragging it on the artboard. To make a perfect square, drag until you see a diagonal magenta line. As you drag, you'll see a tooltip with the dimensions appear on the screen right next to the pointer.

To observe a curving arrow, move the pointer just a little bit away from the bounding box. Drag your square now to rotate it at any angle; if you want to make a diamond shape, hold down Shift and limit the rotation to 45 degrees.

Any of the eight-bounding box handles can be used to scale a shape, and the Transform section of the Properties window makes it simple to adjust the object's dimensions and rotation angle.

Rounding Live Polygon corners

If you would like to round every corner of a polygon, drag the single rounded corner widget. Use the Direct Selection tool to choose a corner widget and click a single corner to change it independently.

Rounding individual corners

If you want to turn a specific corner, double-click one of the Live Corners widgets using the Direct Selection Tool (A). By doing so, a dialog box will appear where you can change the settings for the chosen anchor point.

Choose the Corner: Round option, then choose the Radius size and Rounding style that you want.

Creating and editing ellipses

Hold down the Polygon tool while choosing the Ellipse tool from the toolbar. To make an oval, drag. By sliding the bounding box handles, you can dynamically alter a Live Ellipse's dimensions.

To proportionally resize the form, shift-drag a bounding box handle. To scale proportionally from the center, press Option+Shift on a Mac or Alt+Shift on a Windows computer.

Move the pointer away from a bounding box handle until you see the Rotate icon to rotate an ellipse. Once rotated, drag. The rotation angle is displayed in a tooltip.

Creating and editing circles

Create a new project in Adobe Illustrator with the necessary size before beginning to design a circle in it.

Click on the document's center after choosing the Ellipse tool from the Tools menu.

Then, enter the required radius values in the Radius area, then click OK.

Changing stroke width and alignment

By selecting the Stroke hyperlink in the Control panel, you can open the Illustrator Stroke panel. You can adjust the Width height in the Stroke panel by clicking the Width drop-down box, selecting one of the predefined widths, or by entering a value.

You can accomplish this by using the Escape key. The Stroke panel contains the Align Stroke to Inside button (). The stroke is then positioned so that it is parallel to the rectangles inside edge.

Creating a polygon

To display other nested shape tools, press and hold the Rectangle tool on the toolbar. Drag a shape onto the artboard while using the Polygon tool.

Although the polygon's side widget allows you to dynamically alter the number of sides, the default polygon has six sides. Alternately, utilize the slider or input the desired number of sides by

Clicking More options in the Properties panel's Transform section.

Polygons can be scaled unevenly without losing their living features.

Click Make Sides Equal to convert a form back to a polygon with equal sides.

Editing with a polygon

You can use the Polygon tool to drag a form onto the artboard and edit it with a polygon's us. Six sides are the default for polygons; however, you can adjust this by sliding the side widget. In the Properties panel's Transform section, you can also choose More options and use the slider to set the number of sides.

Creating a star

The "Star tool" is the primary method for making stars in Illustrator, unlike many other actions that may be carried out in a variety of ways. Unless you like to do things the hard way!

In Adobe Illustrator, choose the "Star Tool" from the left toolbar, which is typically next to the "Rectangle Tool."

To define your star, click anywhere on the canvas and change the radius (1 & 2) and the number of points.

Clicking the "Ok" button completes your task.

Drawing lines

Select the Line Segment tool by pressing and holding the Ellipse tool in the toolbar. A tooltip gives instant readouts for the length and angle as you draw a line.

Move the pointer away from an end widget until you see the Rotate icon to rotate the line.

Once rotated, drag. Around its axis, the line revolves.

Using Image Trace to convert images into editable vector art

You may turn raster images (JPEG, PNG, PSD, etc.) into vector art with Image Trace. This tool makes it simple to trace an existing work of art and use it as the basis for a new drawing. For instance, you can use Image Trace to turn the image of a pencil sketch you've made on paper into vector art. To quickly achieve the desired outcome, you can select from a number of tracing presets.

In your Illustrator document, open or insert a raster image.

Choose one of the following actions with the placed image selected:

o To trace using the default settings, select Object > Image Trace > Make. By default, Illustrator turns an image into a black and white trace.

o Choose a preset from the Tracing Presets button, or click the Image Trace button in the Control panel or Properties panel ().

o To open the Image Trace panel, select Window > Image Trace or go to the Tracing workspace, then perform one of the following:

o By tapping the icons on the panel's top, you can select one of the default presets.

o From the Preset drop-down menu, select a preset.

o Indicate the alternatives for tracing.

Adjust the traced results in the Image Trace panel (Window > Image Trace).

Select Object > Image Trace > Expand to turn the tracing object into paths so you may alter the vector artwork by hand.

Cleaning up traced artwork

Using the Type tool to remove stray points and spots where you unintentionally clicked can be quite beneficial.

To quickly clean up your artwork, select Object > Path > Clean Up and then choose what you want to clean up.

Working with drawing modes

The following drawing modes are available in Illustrator:

Draw Normally

Draw Behind

Draw Inside

The Draw Normal mode is the default drawing mode. Under the Color Selector tool in the Tools panel, you can choose several drawing modes.

Click the Drawing Modes panel in the Tools panel, then choose a different drawing mode to cycle through. The Shift+D keyboard shortcut can also be used to switch between drawing modes.

If no artwork is selected, the Draw Behind option enables you to draw behind every piece of content on a chosen layer. If a piece of art is selected, the new object is drawn exactly below it.

As long as you don't select artwork, the Draw Behind option enables you to draw behind every piece of content on a chosen layer. If a piece of art is selected, the new object is drawn exactly below it.

Placing artwork

Because it offers the best amount of file format, positioning, and color support, the Place command is the main way to insert photos into your document. Use the Links panel to locate, pick, keep track of, and update a file once you've placed it.

Avoid copying and pasting images into your document because doing so may result in issues that you won't notice until you go to print.

Take the steps below to place images in Illustrator;

Open the Illustrator document in which you want to have the artwork placed.

Locate the menu bar then select File > Place, then move to the file you want to place.

Click just once on the file this way you won't be looking at the "Link" checkbox.

Ensure that the "Link" checkbox is not checked.

Select the Place option.

Finishing up

When you are done with the postcard take the artwork into position on the artboard earlier described then make some copies of the postcard you have just created.

Select the view option then click on the Fit board option this way you will be able to view the whole artboard at once.

Click on the Selection tool to adjust the objects in the artwork if needed.

Click on the Group button in the properties panel to have the objects on the artwork grouped together. Note that this is only necessary if you have more than one object in the artwork.

Move the object and the text into your preferred position.

You can use the arrange button to make some adjustments to the objects if necessary.

When you are done and satisfied with the way the artboard looks, click on the file option then select save.

Quite another exciting chapter, I am sure by now you have learned all that has to do with creating new documents, creating rectangles and some other basic shapes, creating and editing polygons, creating a star, and also drawing lines. Test your knowledge of the above chapter by taking up the activities below. Ensure you attempt all the questions and if any seem like a tough nut to crack, read through the chapter again and thoroughly this time before attempting again.

Activity

1.How do you create new documents in illustrator?

2.Mention 4 basic shapes in illustrator.

3.How do you round individual corners?

4.How is a polygon created? Draw a polygon of 6 sides pointing out the anchor points.

5.Briefly describe a star tool. Draw a star with the use of the start tool in the toolbar.

6.How are lines drawn in illustrator?

7.Briefly describe how artworks can be placed. Draw two objects while having one behind the other.

Chapter 14: Editing And Combining Shapes And Paths

Starting the lesson

In this lesson, you will be introduced to how to cut and bring shapes and paths together in order to create beautiful artwork which can depict any character of your choice.

Editing paths and shapes

When you use the Pen, Pencil, or Curvature tools to create a route on canvas, it usually consists of one or more straightor curved-line segments.

There are different paths in Illustrator; open paths which is a connected collection of line segments with independent start and endpoints and closed paths, a connected collection of line segments with their beginning and ending points connected to create a shape.

Use the Pen, Pencil, and Curvature tools in the toolbar to draw a path. The Shape Builder tools can be used to construct simple forms. To select a shape tool from the drop-down menu,

Press and hold the Rectangle tool on the toolbar.

Cutting with the Scissors tool

Finding a starting point and an ending point is similar to cutting paper with scissors in that regard. In Illustrator, all you have to do is

Click the two points and then press the delete button as opposed to using actual scissors to cut it all the way through.

Using the Scissors tool, you can cut and delete paths, split shapes in half, or open closed routes.

You must first outline the text because the scissors tool won't operate on the live text. The steps are listed below.

Make a text outline after selecting the text. By pressing Command + Shift + O on the keyboard, you may swiftly outline text.

Choose the Scissors Tool (C). It is accessible from the same menu as the Eraser Tool.

To establish a start, point for the cut, click on the path or anchor point. To clearly observe the anchor points and path, zoom in. A new anchor will show up when you click a path.

From the toolbar, choose the Direct Selection Tool (A).

To remove a line, click on it and press the Delete key. The anchor points can also be moved around to give the text the desired effect.

Joining paths

Improve line quality in Adobe Illustrator. Pathways are joined, extra line segments from overlapping paths are removed, and any openings between two open paths are filled in.

Examine the piece of art; it should contain numerous pathways that ought to be connected. To make aesthetically pleasing artwork, some of these paths need to be linked where they cross, while others contain gaps that need to be filled in.

Add the Join tool to your Basic toolbar before selecting it. At the bottom of the Basic toolbar, select the Edit Toolbar icon (three dots). The All-Tools drawer, which contains all of Illustrator's tools, appears.

You can drag the Join tool anywhere on the toolbar to add it, or you can drag it into a tool group to nest it. Drag it to the toolbar's bottom for the time being.

Find the spot on the piece of art where there is a tiny opening between two paths. Before you join the lines, use the Zoom tool to enlarge your perspective. To join the two pathways, choose the Join tool and doodle a line. By drawing a line connecting two pathways, the Join tool can be used to close a gap.

Cutting with the Knife tool

The knife tool lets you separate portions of a shape or piece of text so that you can make different modifications, split shapes, and cut-out shapes. I particularly enjoy using this tool to create text effects because I can adjust the color and alignment of the different components of the shape.

Build a shape in Adobe Illustrator.

Click on the Knife tool from the toolbar. It is located under the Eraser Tool. Draw through the path you would like to cut it can either be a freehand cut or a straight cut. Note that the path drawn will determine the cut path or shape.

Make use of the selection tool to choose the shape and then edit it.

Cutting in a straight line with the Knife tool

If you will like to cut in a straight line with the knife tool, from step two above;

Hold the Option key (Alt) while you cut through the shape.

Outlining strokes

Strokes can be used for a variety of purposes. They can be bent, reshaped, and shrunk, but the contour cannot be altered like it can with a shape. For instance, while the edges of a rectangle or square can be rounded off, the corners of a stroke cannot. A path with a thick stroke can be easily transformed into an object using the outline stroke so that you can utilize it as a building block in your creations. Adobe Illustrator converts the stroke value of your object into the size of a new shape.

To outline a stroke in an Illustrator, follow the steps below;

Click on File then place and choose an image you would like to place into the Illustrator document.

Open the Appearance panel and then from the Appearance panel flyout menu, click on the Add New Stroke option. Once you have the Stroke option highlighted in the Appearance panel, click on Effect > Path > Outline Object.

Using the Eraser tool

The primary tool for erasing vector shapes in Adobe Illustrator is the Eraser Tool (Shift-E). You can either choose this tool from the toolbar or launch it by

Pressing the Shift-E keyboard shortcut.

Choose the shape you wish to erase before you activate the Erase Tool by pressing the above-discussed control then hold down the Control key while you can make use of the Eraser Tool to choose new shapes.

Erasing in a straight line

With Adobe Illustrator, you can erase clean and in a straight line. To do that simply follow the instructions below;

Tap the spacebar in order to gain access to the Hand tool then move the document in order to see the object you want to erase clearly.

Click on the Selection tool wherein you will click on the tool to make use of.

Click on the view option then Zoom in a few times for a clearer view of the object you are working on.

Click twice on the Eraser Tool in order to edit the tool properties. You can choose to make the Eraser smaller in the Eraser Tool Options dialog box then click on the OK button.

Now that you have chosen the Eraser tool, all you have to do is to move the pointer to where you see the red "X" then tap the Shift key and move straight across to the right side. Let go of the mouse button and the shift key too.

When you are done, click on the File option then click on Save.

Assemble the first dinosaur

Using the dinosaur as an example of an object which you will be arranging, drag the object and position it perfectly on the artboard.

Click on the View option > Fit Artboard In window.

Click on the selection tool and choose any shape of your choice and then have it placed on any part of the artwork (dinosaur).

Creating a compound path

Two or more pathways that cross each other make up a compound path. When you need to expose a portion of an underlying item over a gap in another object, compound routes are employed. On a plate, picture a flat donut. One path determines the doughnut's outer edge, while another one determines the donut hole. Where routes intersect, there is a translucent hole. You can view the plate underneath through this hole. Follow the instructions below to create a compound path;

Choose the paths you would love to include in the compound path.

Click Object then choose the Compound Path option and click on Make.

Combining shapes

Combining shapes can be done with a lot more ease in Illustrator. Simply follow the steps below;

Open the interface and change to the Selection Tool.

Choose your objects by holding down the Shift key to choose various objects.

Click on the Shape Builder or you can also choose to make use of the shortcut Shift + M.

Move your mouse between the objects you would like to combine or merge together.

Once the above step has been completed, let go of the mouse button and the objects will then be merged together.

Start by creating a shape

With Illustrator's vector Shape tools, you may make a wide range of simple shapes. Select the Rectangle tool after pressing and holding the Rectangle tool to see all the Shape tools. Draw a rectangle by dragging it on the artboard. Search for a diagonal magenta guide that depicts a perfect square as you drag.

Working with the Shape Builder tool

The shape builder tool makes it incredibly simple and effective to create shapes, clean up selections, and carry out minute details inside a selection. Let basic forms do the work for you to relieve the stress of having to pen tool everything!

Take the steps below to make use of the Shape Builder tool.

Design the shapes with which you would like to add the Shape Builder tool.

Click on the Selection tool, and choose the paths that you need to combine in order to design the shape. Ensure that just the paths to which you would be applying the tool are selected. If you choose all the paths before you merge then there is likely to be a

Choose the Shape Builder tool from the Tools panel or you can also choose to press the Shift +M key. By default, the tool will be in merge mode so you can merge different paths.

Ensure you identify the region that you want to extract or merge.

If you would like to break or extract the region from the other part of the shape then move the pointer and then click on the chosen region.

If you would like to combine paths, move along the region and then let go of the mouse and the two different regions will then be merged together to create a new shape.

If you would like to make use of the Erase mode of the Shape Builder tool, tap the Alt key (Windows) or click on the Option key (MacOS) then click on the close region that you would like to delete. When you press the Alt key (Windows) or Option key (Mac OS), the pointer will then change to an arrow key.

You can remove portions of specified shapes in the Erase mode. The shapes are broken in such a way that the regions chosen by the marquee are eliminated from the shapes if you delete a region that is shared by numerous objects.

In erase mode, edges can also be deleted. When you need to clear the remaining areas after producing the required shape, this option is helpful.

Assemble the second dinosaur

Remember when we discussed the first dinosaur, now here is another dinosaur to work with.

Take the same positioning step as in the first one and then follow the steps below;

Choose the View option then click on Fit Artboard In Window.

With the use of the Selection tool, move certain pieces into the position as they ought to be, you can choose to download the picture of a dinosaur to work with.

Click on the View option then select the Zoom option in order to zoom into the dinosaur.

If you would like to make a copy of the dinosaur you have assembled, tap the options button then move if you are using a mac or you can tap the Alt key and then move the mouse if you are using Windows. Let go of the mouse button and the key when you have the arrow at the desired position you want to have the object.

Combining objects with the use of Pathfinder effects

The Illustrator Pathfinder Tool is ideal for helping you make a last-minute task appear simple. You may use the tool to manipulate shapes and pathways to speed up your productivity. Because the tool makes it so simple to construct complex shapes, mastering it is crucial. We'll go through the tool's fundamentals in this article to provide you with the knowledge you need to draw exact shapes and paths in your graphics and accelerate your production.

To combine objects with the use of the Pathfinder tool follow the steps below;

Create a new document in Illustrator then choose the shapes you would like to combine.

The Pathfinder panel can be found when you open the Window tab and click on the pathfinder option. You can also make use of the shortcuts by tapping Shift + Ctrl + F9 or you can click on the Shift + Cmd + F9 combinations.

Understanding shape modes

Shape modes change the shape of the final object by combining, omitting, intersecting, or removing individual layers. New and distinctive polygons of a single color are produced by these actions.

Unite

The Unite action joins two or more forms to create a single, well-rounded polygon. This program is perfect for creating and connecting intricate vector objects.

Minus Front

The top shape layers and any overlaps are removed by the Minus Front shape mode, leaving only the bottom shape and color.

Intersect

By exposing the overlapping area and eliminating the top and bottom shape layers, intersecting actions produce a new shape.

Exclude

Using the Exclude shape mode, a complex form is created by removing the overlapped area and leaving behind the remaining polygons.

Reshaping a path

Reshaping a path can never be any easier with the use of Adobe Illustrator.

Follow the instructions below to have your path reshaped;

Select the Direct Selection tool or you can choose to press the A key on the keyboard.

Choose the object in order to view its anchor points and also the path segments.

Click on an anchor point to choose it, or you can choose to press the Shift + Click to choose the multiple anchor points, path segments, or both.

Move the anchor point, handle, or path segment in order to make changes to the shape of your object.

Using the Width tool

You can construct stroke profiles and variable-width strokes with the Width tool to apply styles consistently.

Select the Width tool or you can also press Shift +W to choose it.

Move an anchor point to expand or also contract the stroke.

If you would like to make pointed ends, move the points at the ends of the stroke.

Assemble the last dinosaur

Now we are at the last stage of assembling the dinosaur.

Click on the View option the click on Fit Artboard In Window.

Click on the Selection tool to move any part of the dinosaur.

Click on the View option then Zoom in to get a clearer view.

Move the object to your preferred position.

If you would like to make a copy of the reshaped path, tap on the option key then move the mouse if you are using a mac or you can tap the Alt key while also moving the mouse if you are using windows.

You must agree with me by now that Adobe Illustrator is a fun tool to use. Most times when it comes to designing, I am always in a fix choosing between Photoshop and Illustrator.

In the just concluded chapter, you must have learned how to edit shapes, and make use of the scissors tool, knife tool, and eraser tool. You must have also learned how to join paths and create compound paths.

Don't just assume you know all the chapter contains, take the activity below and ensure you complete it all by yourself.

Activity

1.State how paths and shapes can be edited.

2.Briefly describe what the scissors and knife tool is.

3.Can different paths be joined? If yes, briefly describe how.

4.How can shapes be combined? Combine a square and a circle together.

5.What are shapes modes?

6.Briefly describe the width tool.

7.Draw any shape of your choice and erase the upper path in a straight line.

Chapter 15: Transforming Artwork

How do you transform your artwork to make it very unique and quite amazing? This chapter will introduce you to this and you would also learn how to add, edit, rename, and also reorder artboards in an existing document, you will learn to navigate artboards, work with rulers and guides, position objects with accurate precision, explore mirror repeat, etc.

Starting the lesson

You can rapidly and precisely alter an artwork's size, shape, and orientation as you work on it. As you create many pieces of artwork in this session, you'll learn about creating and editing artboards, the various Transform commands, and specialized tools.

Working with artboards

You can speed up the design process and work on designs on an endless canvas with artboards. An artboard in Illustrator functions as the canvas for your creative work, much like a blank piece of white paper would. To develop your artwork, you can construct custom-sized artboards or use the presets for common devices that are given. They can also be printed or exported.

The setting and size of your artboard are selectable in Illustrator when you start a new document or open an existing one. You can add or make several artboards if you have multiple designs. Additionally, you can change the size, name, duplicate, and remove an artboard to suit your needs.

Drawing a custom-sized artboard

Creating a new artboard

Consider that you wish to expand your design, export it, or print it on several pages. You can build multiple artboards in a single document rather than multiple ones. The Artboard tool can be used to build an artboard.

Select the Artboard tool in the tool panel or you can choose to press the Shift + O key.

If you would like to add preset or custom dimensions make use of the artboard options or you can also choose to press the Esc key if you would like to leave the artboardediting mode.

To add preset or custom dimensions, make use of the artboard options or you can also press the Esc key to leave the artboard-editing mode.

Editing artboards

You might want to resize, rename, duplicate, delete, or manage artboards when working with designs on several artboards to give your artwork a practical arrangement. An artboard's name appears in its upper-left corner.

Make sure the Artboard tool is chosen if you want to resize, rename, or duplicate an artboard.

Resize the artboard

Choose the artboard and then move the bounding box to change the size of the artboard then do the following

o Locate the Artboards panel then click on the More Options the choose the Artboard Options.

o Fix the reference points or you can also choose to indicate the required width and height of your board.

Rename artboard

Choose one or more artboards.

In the artboards panel, click on More options > Duplicate Artboards.

Press the Esc key to leave the artboard editing mode.

Copying artboards between artboards

You should manage your artboards after you develop them and adjust them to meet your design requirements. If your artboards have a lot of designs and layers, organizing them will help you arrange your concepts and designs.

Your artboards can be easily moved across papers or within your project by cutting, copying, and pasting. There are numerous methods to arrange or reorder your artboards in Illustrator. You can also change the view of your artboard and read more about the extra artboard options.

To quickly duplicate your drawings, you can cut, copy, and paste artboards between Illustrator documents or inside the same document. Similar to moving text, you can transfer artboards to any location inside the same document or another.

Select the Artboard tool.

Choose one or more artboards.

To cut or copy and paste the artboard into the same or another document, press Ctrl + X, Ctrl + C, or Ctrl + V.

Aligning and arranging artboards

Object alignment definitely gives the scene a neat and organized appearance. Instead of doing it by hand, which would require perfect accuracy, in a matter of clicks, the Align panel can produce the optimal outcome.

You may easily reposition your artwork with the help of the Align tools in Adobe Illustrator. You can maintain accuracy and organization in your work by understanding how to align things. And it takes less than two minutes to complete.

Without moving the artboards about in the workspace, you can alter the artboard order when you export or print an Illustrator document. You would need to reorganize artboards in order to organize them in the workspace. Depending on your arrangement, you can reposition your artboards in any number of columns or rows. You can organize your thought process and export your artboard sequentially by rearranging the artboards.

Setting options for artboards

Follow these steps to use the Artboard options:

Double-click your artboard after selecting the Artboard tool.

Give your artboard a name in the Artboard Options dialog and choose one of the following actions:

From the Preset drop-down menu, pick an option.

To change the artboard's width and height, enter values in the W and H fields.

To set the Orientation of your artboard, choose Landscape or Portrait.

Reordering artboards

Without moving the artboards about in the workspace, you can alter the artboard order when you export or print an Illustrator document. You would need to reorganize artboards in order to organize them in the workspace. Depending on your arrangement, you can reposition your artboards in any number of columns or rows. You can organize your thought process and export your artboard sequentially by rearranging the artboards.

To reorder artboards, do one of the following;

Select the Artboard tool.

Locate the Artboards panel then click on the Up and Down arrows.

Working with rulers and guides

Rulers enable precise placement and measurement of objects in an artboard or illustration window. The ruler origin is the location where 0 appears on each ruler.

Separate rulers for documents and artboards are provided by Illustrator. Only one of these rulers can be chosen at once. In the image window's top and left corners, there are global rulers. The top-left corner of the illustration window is where the default ruler origin is situated.

On the top and left sides of the active artboard, rulers are visible. The top-left corner of the artboard is where the default artboard ruler origin is situated.

When you choose artboard rulers instead of global rulers, the origin point adjusts to correspond with the currently active artboard. For artboard rulers, you can also choose a different origin point. The pattern fills in objects on the artboards are now unaffected by changing the origin of the artboard ruler.

The upper-left corner of the first artboard serves as the default origin point for the global ruler, and the top-left corner of each individual artboard serves as the default origin point for each individual artboard ruler.

Select View > Rulers > Show Rulers or View > Rulers > Hide Rulers to reveal or conceal rulers.

To switch between artboard rulers and global rulers, select view the click on rulers > Switch to Global Rulers or View > Rulers > Change to Artboard Rulers. Note that Artboard rulers will be displayed by default hence the Change to Global Rulers option will be displayed in the submenu of the Ruler.

If you would like to display or hide video rulers, click on the View option > Show Video Rulers or View > Hide Video Rulers.

To make changes to the ruler origin, drag the pointer to the upper left corner where you have the ruler intersecting then move the pointer to the exact position where you would like the new ruler appearing.

To restore the default ruler origin, click twice on the upper left corner where the ruler intersects.

Creating guides

If the ruler is not being displayed currently, click on the View option then click on show rulers.

Place the pointer on the left ruler so as to have a vertical guide or you can also choose to place it at the top ruler for a perfect horizontal guide.

Move the guide to the preferred position.

If you would like to place a restriction on the guides to an artboard rather than having it on the whole canvas, choose the Artboard tool and move the guides to the artboard.

Move, delete or release guides

If guides happen locked, click on view then Guides > Lock Guides.

Once the above step has been completed, you can then choose to do any of the following;

o To move the guide, you can simply copy it and have it pasted in the desired location.

o To have guides deleted, tap the backspace key for windows or the Delete key for Mac users.

o If you would like to delete the guide all at once, click on View > Guides > Clear Guides.

When you create, modify, or work with objects or artboards, Smart Guides temporary snap-to guides appear. Through snap-alignment and display of X, Y positions, and delta values, they assist you in aligning, editing, and transforming objects or artboards in relation to other objects, artboards, or both. By adjusting the Smart Guides options, you can choose the specific smart guides and feedback that are displayed (such as measurement labels, object highlighting, or labels). Note that by default, Smart Guides are on.

Transforming content

Moving, turning, reflecting, scaling, and shearing are all examples of transformation.

Object > Transform commands, the Transform panel, specialist tools, and other methods can all be used to transform objects.

By dragging the bounding box for a selection, you can also make a variety of alterations.

When you are copying items, you may occasionally want to repeat the same transformation more than once. You can repeat a move, scale, rotate, reflect, or shear operation as many times as you like with the Transform Again command in the Object menu, up until you use a different transform operation.

Information on the position, scale, and orientation of one or more selected items is shown in the Transform panel (Window > Transform). You can change the selected objects' pattern fills, their selections, or both by entering new values. Additionally, you can lock the object's proportions and alter the transformation reference point.

Except for the X and Y values, which refer to the chosen reference point, all values in the panel refer to the bounding boxes of the objects. Check the Align to Pixel Grid checkbox to pixel-align individual items.

Working with the bounding box

The Bounding Box in Adobe Illustrator is an interactive selection that shows you have chosen a certain object. You can scale, shear, rotate, and move the chosen item with this tool.

Typically, the bounding box starts out as a rectangular shape with sides that are perpendicular to the vertical and horizontal axes.

Reset Bounding Box in Illustrator is grayed out because some shapes and lines are incompatible with the feature.

Click on the shape to bring up the menu, then select Object > Shape > Expand Shape to correct the situation. The bounding box should now be able to be reset.

Positioning artwork using the Properties panel

Illustrator's Properties panel enables you to view settings and controls in relation to the task or workflow you are currently working on. You can reach the appropriate controls whenever you need them thanks to this panel's user-friendly design.

In the Essentials workspace, the Properties panel is automatically accessible. Additionally, it can be found under Window > Properties.

Each Properties panel area's frequently used controls are shown upfront. By clicking an option that is underlined or the ellipses in the lower-right corner of a section, you can access further controls.

To position the artwork, flow the instructions below;

Click on the View option then click on the Fit All in Window to see all three artboards.

Click in the blank artboard in the middle so it becomes the active artboard.

Click to choose the group of artworks with the Untouched Beauty text that can be found beneath the artboards. There might be a need for you to zoom out or pan in order t be able to see it.

When in the Transform section of the Properties panel, select the upper-left point of the reference point locator. Make changes to the X value and the Y value (you can choose to set them at 0) then click on Return or Tap the Enter button.

To reduce the size of the chosen piece of art, hold down the Shift key while dragging. Verify that the pink rectangle in the backdrop is precisely the right size for the artboard. Other pieces of art may protrude, but that's good.

Click on Select > Deselect then click on File > Save.

Scaling objects precisely

When an item is scaled, it can be increased or decreased vertically (along the y axis), horizontally (along the x-axis), or both. Depending on the method you select for scaling, objects are scaled in relation to a certain reference point. Most scaling techniques allow you to alter the default reference point, and you can also lock an object's dimensions. You can scale objects with the scale tool, and bounding box, and you can also scale multiple objects at the same time.

Rotating objects with the Rotate tool

When you rotate an object, it revolves around the designated fixed point. The center of the item serves as the default reference point. Numerous objects in a selection will rotate around a single reference point, which is by default the center of the selection or bounding box if there are multiple objects in the selection. Using the Transform Each command, you can rotate each item around its own center point.

To rotate an object with the use of the rotate tool follow the instructions below;

Choose one or more objects.

Choose the Rotate tool option. You can then do any of the following;

o Drag the item in a circular motion anywhere in the document window to rotate it around its center point.

o Click once anywhere in the document window to move the reference point and rotate the object around a new point of reference. Then drag the cursor in a circular motion while moving it away from the reference location.

o After you begin dragging, hold down Alt (Windows) or Option (Mac OS) to rotate a replica of the object rather than the original.

Scale using Transform Each

A Transformation Instead of using a single reference point, each command enables you to transform numerous objects about each of their unique reference points. You can scale or move objects horizontally or vertically, rotate them at a specified degree, or make a mirror image of them with the Transform Each command. You can also ask Illustrator to perform random modifications if you want to produce a distinctive result. Similar effects can be created and modified using the Transform Effect command.

To make use of the transform each command;

Choose the Selection tool on the Tools panel.

Choose one or more objects you would like to transform.

Click on the object menu the direct the arrow at Transform them click on the Transform Each option.

Click on the Preview option in the check box after which you can either choose to scale horizontal or vertical, move horizontal or vertical, rotate angle, or reflect X or Y.

Finally, click on the OK button or you can also choose to copy.

Shearing objects

Shearing an object causes it to skew or slant along the horizontal, vertical, or at a specific angle with respect to an axis. Depending on the shearing method you select, objects shear relative to a reference point that can be altered for the majority of shearing methods. When shearing one or more items at once, you can lock one dimension of the object being sheared. Shearing of objects can be done with ease with the use of the shear command.

Transforming with the Free Transform tool

The Free Transform tool enables you to edit photos and objects. The Free Transform tool, for instance, allows you to rotate, reflect, shear, or resize art.

Using repeats

With only one click, Illustrator enables you to quickly repeat items and change their styles. Simply construct the first object and select a repeat type that is all that is required (Radial, Grid, or Mirror). The entire artwork will be automatically generated for you using Illustrator. Repeats can also be easily changed; all instances automatically update to reflect the change after one item is updated. There are about three different types of repeats which are; radial repeat, grid repeat, and mirror repeat.

Applying a mirror repeat

Illustrator will automatically construct the opposite half of the symmetrical artwork for you after you complete the first half.

Making a mirror repeat

Create the first part of the artwork, then use the Selection tool to make a selection. Grid > Object > Repeat.

The object is repeated using the default options for a grid repeat type.

Editing a mirror repeat

To rotate or change the mirrored portion, drag the handles below or above the original piece of art.

To adjust the angle and distance between the two pieces of art, move the symmetry axis between them.

When done, the control handles are not visible if you click elsewhere and then click again. The artwork's two sides are grouped together and move as one unit. Double-click the artwork to edit them once again.

Using grid and radial repeats

Grid

With only one click, create artwork that calls for repeated elements in an array.

Making a grid repeat

Make the object, then use the Selection tool to make the selection. Grid > Object > Repeat.

The object is repeated using the default options for a grid repeat type.

Radial

You can quickly produce artwork that calls for repeated elements around a circle, akin to a wheel's spokes with the radial option.

You can make a radial repeat by;

Make the object, then use the Selection tool to make the selection.

Select-Object, Repeat, and Radial.

The item is repeated using the default options for a radial repeat type.

Adding the Puppet Warp tool to the toolbar

The Puppet Warp tool in Illustrator makes it simple to bend and reposition graphics into multiple configurations.

At the bottom of the toolbar, select Edit Toolbar (Icon shows three dots in a row inside a rectangle box). Drag the Puppet Warp tool (Icon of puppet warp tool.) between two tools in the toolbar, and if necessary, scroll through the menu that appears.

To make the extra tools menu disappear, press the Escape key.

Adding pins and Rotating pins

You may bend and warp elements of your artwork using Puppet Warp so that the changes seem natural. The Puppet Warp tool in Illustrator allows you to add, move, and rotate pins to easily change the appearance of your artwork.

Practice Question

1.What is an artboard?

2.Can artboards be edited once they have been created? If yes, describe how.

3.How can artboards be aligned and arranged?

4.What is a bounding box?

5.What is a mirror repeat and how can it be applied?

6.What is a radial repeat?

7.How can the puppet warp tool be added to the toolbar?

Chapter 16: Using The Basic Drawing Tools

Drawing is definitely done better with the use of the illustrator. That being said, there are some very basic drawing tools that you need to familiarize yourself with. In this lesson you will learn how to; draw curves and straight lines with the use of the curvature tool, edit paths with the curvature tool, create dashed lines, draw and also edit with the use of the pencil tool, and lots more.

Starting the lesson

You will begin this lesson by creating free-form paths with straight lines, and smooth and refined curves.

Creating with the Curvature tool

The Curvature tool makes drawing simple and intuitive while also making path building easier. You can create, toggle, edit, add, or remove smooth or corner points using this tool. To work swiftly and precisely with pathways, you don't need to switch between multiple tools.

Click on the curvature tool.

Bring down two points on the artboard, and then view the rubber band preview to display the shape of the resulting path based on the very place where you hover your mouse.

Make use of the mouse in dropping a point or you can also choose to tap to design a smooth point. If you would like to design a corner point, simply click twice or you can also choose to press the Alt key while you are either tapping or clicking.

Drawing paths with the Curvature tool

Simply click once to establish the initial anchor point with the Curvature tool chosen. You'll observe that clicking and dragging cause the anchor points you're going to draw to move. You'll notice that Illustrator is calculating the necessary curve between the two anchor points you just made as you click to create the second anchor point and the location of your mouse as you move it as you click. To help you understand how to make a specific shape, I've traced it in the figure below. As you can see, I've set up two anchor points along the path I'm trying to draw, and as I move the mouse, the path's curvature is calculated based on where the mouse is located.

As the Curvature tool determines the curve necessary to connect each anchor point, keep clicking to add anchor points intermittently along the path. Prior anchor points can be moved by clicking and dragging them to a new spot as you draw or trace your path. You'll notice as you go how the curve of the line segment between the anchor points is impacted by the adjustment. The Curvature tool will let you click the anchor point you initially created to end the path when you return to it (note the circle next to your cursor).

The Curvature tool closes the route by default with a portion of a curved line, which may not be what you want. However, by double-clicking the initial anchor point, you can construct a corner point, which is then used to create straight line segments. Any anchor point you construct can be double-clicked to switch between a corner point (straight line segment) and a smooth point (curved line segment).

Drawing a river path

This section introduces you to how you can draw a river path with the use of the curvature tool.

You will begin by drawing one side of the river then you proceed to draw the other side of the river.

Drag the pointer over the horizon path and then right-click and let go of the mouse to begin a new path.

Move the pointer down and to the left side then you can right-click once again. Continue to drag the pointer downwards then click and make changes to the direction to create the first side of the river. When you are just getting to make use of the curvature tool, it helps to learn how to click and then release the mouse for the pointer to move faster.

Tap the escape key which will make you stop drawing a path.

Employ all the steps above in drawing the other side of the river.

Click on Select then Deselect.

Note that it is best to have an artwork depicting a river downloaded, with this you will be able to follow the artwork when you are drawing with the curvature tool.

Editing a path with the Curvature tool

With the Curvature tool, you can modify pathways by moving, deleting, or adding new anchor points. Regardless of the drawing tool used to generate it, you can adjust any path you've made or are currently creating with the Curvature tool.

To edit with the use of the curvature tool simply;

Select the Curvature tool in the toolbar then click twice on an anchor point this way you will convert it between a corner and a smooth point.

If you would like to remove a selected point all you have to do is to press the Delete key for Mac or press the backspace key for windows.

Creating corners with the Curvature tool

The Curvature tool by default produces smooth anchor points or anchor points that bend the path. Corner points and smooth points are the two types of anchor points that can be used on paths. A path abruptly changes direction at a corner. Path segments are joined into a continuous curve at a smooth point.

You may also make corner points to make straight routes using the Curvature tool.

Select the curvature tool then move the pointer over the left side of the path.

Drag the pointer up and then to the right side this way you will be creating a corner you can then move the pointer down and to the right also and then click to create a new point.

Drag the pointer to the top of the anchor point on the chosen path and when the pointer changes to an arrow sign you can then click twice to change it to a corner point.

Press the escape key to leave when you are done drawing. Note that making a corner point just needs you to click twice on the anchor point.

Click on the Select option > Deselect then click on File > Save.

Creating dashed lines

Create your line first using the Line Tool () or the Pen Tool (P).

Holding down the Shift key while clicking and dragging with the Line Tool () makes it simple to draw a straight line. The Line Segment Tool Options window can also be opened by clicking on your artboard. Click OK to construct the line after setting its Angle and Length.

Click once to add the line's starting point with the Pen Tool (P), and then hold down Shift to draw a straight line. Click again to add the second end of the line, and then hit Escape to complete the route creation and move to the Selection Tool (V).

Open the Stroke panel by choosing Window > Stroke while ensuring that your line is still selected. Open the fly-out menu from the Stroke panel and select Show Possibilities if you can't see all the options in the following image.

Select the Dashed Line option from the Stroke panel to create a dashed line. Your line will become dashed if the first Dash value is set to 12 points by default. To make each dash easier to see, increase the value for the first gap setting to 20 points (or more).

Creating with the Pencil tool

One of Illustrator's most potent drawing tools is the Pen tool, which can be found on the Toolbar. It allows you to make and alter pathways and anchor points.

Start by selecting the Pen Tool in the Toolbar and setting the stroke weight to 1 point, the color to black, and the fill to none in the Properties window.

Drawing paths with the Pencil tool

To draw a path with the use of the pencil tool simply follow the instructions below;

Select two pencils from the Artboard Navigation menu in the lower-left corner of the Document window.

Choose the pencil tool from the paintbrush tool group that can be found in the toolbar.

Click twice on the pencil tool then in the Pencil Tool Options dialog box, set the following options;

o Move the fidelity slider to the right to smooth. With this, the path will be smooth, and also the number of points drawn with the pencil tool will be reduced.

Click on the OK button. Then move the arrow towards the document window and an asterisk will be displayed indicating that you are about to create a path. You can then draw a path from this position.

Note that you can also choose to redraw the path by simply moving the pointer on or near the previously drawn path. When the asterisk close to the path that indicates that a path is about to be drawn disappears, press and move the pointer to reshape the path ensuring that the pointer begins on the original path and goes back to it before the mouse is released.

Drawing straight lines with the Pencil tool

When using the Pen tool,

Click once, then let go to create an anchor point.

You may see a preview of the path you are making as you move the pointer. Another anchor point can be made by clicking and releasing. To add more anchor points for the path, keep clicking and releasing in different locations.

Move the pointer over the initial anchor point to close a route, then click the endpoint while holding down the Shift key when a circle appears next to the pointer. Press the Escape key to end sketching a path without closing it.

Joining with the Join tool

The Join tool will initially be added to your Basic toolbar. At the bottom of the Basic toolbar, select the Edit Toolbar icon (three dots). The All-Tools drawer, which contains all of Illustrator's tools, emerges.

You can drag the Join tool anywhere on the toolbar to add it, or you can drag it into a tool group to nest it. Drag it to the toolbar's bottom for the time being.

Finishing the Camp logo

Follow the steps below to finish up with the camp log;

Select the View option then click on Fit Artboard In Window.

Choose the Selection tool, and select the shape of your choice.

If you would like to drag the shape on top of the other artwork you are working on, select the Arrange button in the Properties panel then click on Bring to Font.

Ensure you align the shapes and make sure they are a perfect fit.

Create a camp text logo and have it designed just the way you want then move it to the other part of the logo.

Select the Swap button from the stroke panel to swiftly change the start and bring to an end arrowhead in Illustrator.

Use the Scale values from the Stroke panel to bring an adjustment to the size of your start and end arrowhead in Illustrator.

To position the arrow tip at the end of the route or to extend it past the end of the path, use the Align buttons from the Stroke panel.

Adding arrowheads to the paths

The Stroke panel (Window > Stroke) in Illustrator is the most popular method for drawing arrows.

Any open path is easily transformable into an arrow. Simply choose it, make sure a stroke is applied, then pick the Arrowheads options in the Stroke panel.

Use the Stroke panel's Align buttons to position the arrow tip at the end of the path or to extend it past the end of the path.

Remember that you may use Illustrator to make a double-ended arrow by choosing different arrow designs at either end of the path.

Activity

1.What is the curvature tool and how is it used?

2.Briefly highlight the steps that can be taken in drawing a river path.

3.Can a corner be created with the use of the curvature tool? If so, how?

4.List the steps that should be taken when drawing straight lines with a pencil.

5.Draw a straight line with the use of a pencil tool.

6.What is a joining tool?

7.How can arrowheads be added to paths?

Chapter 17: Drawing With The Pen Tool

The pen tool is a very useful tool in illustrator that is used to draw straight and curved lines with the Pen tool, edit curved and straight lines and also add and delete anchor points.

Starting the lesson

In this lesson, I will introduce you to how to create paths with the Pen tool.

Why use the 'Pen' tool?

You can also draw straight and curved pathways with the Pen tool (a symbol of a pen), but you have even more control over the path's shape.

The Pen tool can be used to alter artwork you generate with other drawing tools as well as to create fresh vector artwork that needs greater precision.

What can you create with the pen tool?

You click to add anchor points while using the Pen tool. A straight line can be constructed by making two points.

You press and drag to establish an anchor point with direction lines when using the Pen tool to draw a curve. You may precisely regulate the length and incline of the path entering and exiting an anchor point using anchor point direction lines.

Direction lines are automatically generated when you use the Curvature tool or the Pencil tool to draw curves, but you can't see or work with them while using those tools to draw.

Starting with the pen tool

Anchor points are the main focus of the pen tool. You are connecting anchor points by drawing lines or shapes. To design any shape you want, you can draw straight lines, and curved lines, and add or remove anchor points.

Start creating by choosing the Pen Tool from the toolbar or by pressing the letter P on the keyboard.

Creating straight lines to make a crown

To start, use the Pen tool to draw straight lines to form the primary route of a royal crown, similar to the one you can see at the top of the first artboard.

From the toolbar, choose the Pen tool (a pen icon).

The Fill color box in the Properties panel should be clicked. Make sure the Swatches option (Icon of Swatches option) is chosen in the panel that appears, then choose None (Icon of a square with a diagonal in red).

Make sure the color black is selected in the Stroke box by clicking it. Ensure that the properties panel's stroke weight is set to 1 point as well.

It's typically advisable to leave the path's fill empty when drawing with the Pen tool because it can accidentally cover up some of the path's intended shape. If you need to, you can add a fill afterward.

Notice the asterisk next to the Pen icon (an icon of a pen tool pointer with an asterisk sign at the bottom right.), signifying that you'll establish a new route if you start sketching when you move the pointer into the region designated "Work Area" on the artboard.

Place the cursor over the labeled gray dot. Create an anchor point by clicking and releasing. You simply paved a straight road. A path is made up of two anchor points and the line segment across them. A corner point is the kind of anchor point you just produced. Instead of being smooth like a curve, corner points produce an angle at the anchor point. The Pen tool automatically produces corner points and straight lines, unlike the Curvature tool.

You can also choose to have a crown picture close by so you know the line and paths that you should draw.

Adding some color to the crown

Locate the Properties panel and select the Fill color box to add some colors to the crown you just made.

Choose a color fill from the panel that appears.

Click on the File option then click on Save.

Selecting and editing paths in the crown

This is similar to the previous lesson where you learned how to edit paths, all you have to do is to follow the same procedure.

Click on the Direct Selection tool.

Move the pointer then click to choose the anchor point.

Move the anchor point you must have chosen in such a way that it rearranges it.

Move the Direct Selection pointer over the paths then click on the Edit option > Cut.

Drawing house with the Pen tool

By now you must have learned how to draw with the pen tool, here you will be drawing a house with the pen tool.

Follow the steps below to get this done;

Locate the Artboard Navigation menu in the lower-left corner of the Document window.

Click on the Zoom tool in the toolbar then choose the area that is labeled "Work Area" that can be found in the artboard to zoom in.

Select the View menu then click on the Smart Guides to have them turned on.

Select the pen tool in the properties panel and ensure that the fill color is set to none.

Move the arrow to the main anchor that is close to the pointer you can then click to set another anchor with which you would be using to get the house drawn.

Ensure you set various points on the artboard and also make sure the points are labeled; this point is the exact place from which you will begin to draw the house.

Click on the View option then choose Smart Guides in order to turn off the Smart Guides. Once the guide is off, you can then press the Shift key in order to ensure the points align.

Connect all of the anchor points together with which you will be able to complete the house structure.